THE BIG COUNTRY COOKBOOK

THE BIG COUNTRY COOKBOOK

Recipes and Histories from Sixteen Counties in West Texas

Happy Birthday Mr. C

TIFFANY HARELIK

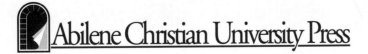

Abilene Christian University Press

BIG COUNTRY COOKBOOK

Recipes and Histories from Sixteen Counties in West Texas

ACU
PRESS

Copyright © 2017 by Tiffany Harelik

ISBN 978-0-89112-420-7

Printed in the United States of America

Cover and interior text design by Sandy Armstrong, Strong Design

For information contact:
Abilene Christian University Press
ACU Box 29138
Abilene, Texas 79699

1-877-816-4455
www.acupressbooks.com

17 18 19 20 21 22 / 7 6 5 4 3 2 1

This book is dedicated to everyone who loves the Big Country area of Texas. May this collection honor the communities represented, reflect their kindheartedness, and share their great recipes.

Table of Contents

Foreword: Lisa and Tom Perini 11

Preface 13

Introduction 17

Road Trip through the Big Country

Football in the Big Country: 33
    Hugh Sandifer

Steak in the Big Country: 37
    Jason Holloway

Growing Food in the Big Country: 41
    Mike Hardwick

Bear Branch 49

The Mill 59

Lola's in Buffalo Gap 85

A West Texas Original: The Texas Cowboys' Christmas Ball 117

The Salad Buffet: Doris Jackson 175

The Beehive 179

Recipes

Beverages

AA's Egg Nog 47
    Jane Bonner, Cross Plains

Big Country Sunset Margaritas 51
    Katie Browning, Abilene

Easy Wassail 52
    Connie Kirkham, Cross Plains

Rosealea Bonner's Shower Punch 53
    Jean McWilliams, Cross Plains

Sherbet Punch 54
    Connie Kirkham, Cross Plains

Strawberry Cherry Basil Lemonade 55
    Tiffany Harelik, Buffalo Gap/Cross Plains

Texas Milk Punch 56
    Elizabeth Wagstaff, Abilene

The Mill Wineritas 57
    Bridget McDowell, Aspermont/Abilene

Breakfasts

Betty Jim's Cheese Blintzes 62
    Betty Jim Parks Harelik, Comanche, via
    Tiffany Harelik

Breakfast Braid 64
    Connie Kirkham, Cross Plains

Breakfast Bundt Cake 66
    Roxie Thomas, Cross Plains

Breakfast Cups 67
    Connie Kirkham, Cross Plains

Christmas Morning Coffee Cake 68
    Martha Minter Ferguson, Abilene

Cinnamon Waffles 69
    Connie Kirkham, Cross Plains

Connie's Breakfast Casserole 70
    Connie Kirkham, Cross Plains

Mer's Sausage Egg Casserole 71
    Jessica Melson, Abilene

Poppy Seed Sausage Rolls 72
Melanie Brown, Abilene

Tomato Florentine Quiche 74
Connie Kirkham, Cross Plains

Breads

Chuck Wagon Sourdough Biscuits 76
Cowboy Museum, Stamford, via Sandra Rhea

Granny's Banana Nut Bread 77
Connie Kirkham, Cross Plains

Healthy, Yummy Muffins 78
Kaye Price-Hawkins, Abilene

Jimmy's Thanksgiving Rolls 81
Dr. Jimmy Harelik,
Comanche/Cross Plains

Mexican Corn Bread 82
Connie Kirkham, Cross Plains

Navajo Fry Bread 83
Lola Molina, Buffalo Gap

Potato Refrigerator Rolls 86
Willie May Rider, Early

Refrigerator Rolls 87
Mary Frances Morgan, De Leon, via Kay
Harelik Morgan

Appetizers and Snacks

Baked Sandwiches 90
Jane Bonner, Cross Plains

Cheese Straws 91
Doris Jackson via Gavin Jackson, Abilene

Chorizo-Stuffed, Bacon-Wrapped Dates . . . 92
Tiffany Harelik, Buffalo Gap/Cross Plains

Guacamole 93
Jane Bonner, Cross Plains

Olive Dip 94
Kaye Price-Hawkins, Abilene

Oysters 95
Jane Bonner, Cross Plains

Pecan Cheese Ball 96
The Texas Cowboys' Christmas Ball, Anson

Pimiento Cheese 97
Tiffany Harelik, Buffalo Gap/Cross Plains

Sausage Balls 98
Doris Jackson via Gavin Jackson, Abilene

Southwest Cheesecake Appetizer 99
Katie Browning, Abilene

Sweet and Sour Tapenade 101
Melanie Brown, Abilene

Thelma's Tuna-Stuffed Jalapeños 102
Sam Waring, Comanche

Sauces and Jellies

Debbie's BBQ Baste 104
Debbie McInroe, Rising Star

Dried Fruit Compote 107
Sheila Wells of Brennan Vineyards,
Comanche

George's Barbecue Sauce 109
George L. Minter Jr., Abilene, via Martha
Minter Ferguson

Green Pepper Jelly 110
Jean McWilliams, Rising Star

Picante Sauce 111
Katie Browning, Abilene

Plum Jam 112
Ellen Webb via Carol Dromgoole, Albany/
Abilene

Soups and Stews

Battalion Beef Soup 114
The Texas Cowboys' Christmas Ball, Anson

Beef Stew 115
Connie Kirkham, Cross Plains

Chicken and Dumplings 116
The Texas Cowboys' Christmas Ball, Anson

Comanche Stew 120
Sam Waring, Comanche

Easy Potato Soup 123
Jessica Melson, Abilene

Lazy Eight Stew 124
Cathy Allen, Coleman

Potato Leek Soup 125
Mary Powell, Abilene

Sides

Acorn Squash Mash 128
Olivia Clardy Tyler, Abilene

Beth Morgan's Seven-Layer Salad 130
Beth Morgan, De Leon, via Kay Harelik
Morgan

Broccoli Rice Casserole 131
Willie May Rider, Early

Corn Casserole.............................. 132
Kaye Price-Hawkins, Abilene

Cranberry Salsa............................ 133
Loretta Newberry, Potosi, via Emily Gilmore

Jessica's Favorite Green Chile Hominy ... 134
Perini Ranch Steakhouse, Buffalo Gap

Maggie's Salad............................. 135
Maggie Meers, Hamby

Maw Maw Harelik's Cottage Cheese
Side Dish.............................. 136
Kay Harelik Morgan, Comanche

Paw's Squash Dressing 137
Elizabeth Hiller via Emily Gilmore, Abilene

Potluck Grape Salad 138
Tiffany Harelik, Buffalo Gap/Cross Plains

Rafter 3 Beans............................ 139
Mary Miller via Susan Allen, Coleman

Roasted Brussels Sprouts 140
Carla Garrett, Abilene

Roasted Sweet Potatoes 141
Roxie Thomas, Cross Plains

Rustic Corn Pudding 142
The Texas Cowboys' Christmas Ball, Anson

Squash Casserole 143
Paulette Foster, Cross Plains

Sweet Potato Casserole................... 144
Margaret Henderson, Coleman

Veggie Pack............................... 145
Mike and Janna Hardwick, Rising Star

Main Courses

Alaskan Salmon Salad.................... 148
Paulette Foster, Cross Plains

Alice Roby's Dove 151
Connie Kirkham, Cross Plains

Barbecued Brisket 152
The Texas Cowboys' Christmas Ball, Anson

Brent's Brisket in the Oven............... 153
Brent Bush via Hailie Harelik Hubbard, Early

Chicken and Wild Rice.................... 154
Mary Powell, Abilene

David's Perfect Texas Brisket............. 157
David McInroe, Rising Star

Ellen Webb's Fried Chicken 158
Ellen Webb via Carol Dromgoole, Albany/
Abilene

Family-Style Sausage and Peppers....... 160
Jerrod Medulla, Abilene

Italian Stewed Pork Chops 162
Tiffany Prier Lamb and Judy Voelter, Abilene

Lasagna to Die For 164
Angie Wiley, Abilene

Mamie's Party Hamburgers 166
Mary Pittman Minter, Abilene, via Martha
Minter Ferguson

Mom's Spaghetti.......................... 167
Katie Browning, Abilene

Parmesan Chicken 168
Ellen Webb via Carol Dromgoole, Albany/
Abilene

Patty's Enchilada Stack................... 169
Patty Rogers, Hawley

Poppy Seed Chicken 171
Julia Porter Bramblett, Abilene

Quail on the Grill 172
Connie Kirkham, Cross Plains

Rosealea's Chicken Salad 173
Jean McWilliams, Cross Plains

Scrambled Hamburger Salad 174
Doris Jackson via Gavin Jackson, Abilene

Shredded Beef Tacos...................... 176
Maggie Meers, Hamby

Slow Cooker Enchiladas................... 177
Jami Anders, Rule/Abilene, via Stephanie
Anders Hood, Abilene

The Beehive's Chicken Fried Chicken 178
Nariman Esfaniary and Aaron Perez, Abilene

Turkey, Dressing, and Gravy.............. 181
Ellen Webb via Carol Dromgoole, Albany/
Abilene

Venison Bourguignon 183
Brennan Vineyards, Comanche

Venison over Noodles..................... 186
Connie Kirkham, Cross Plains

Venison Piccata 187
Erin Maloney Schroeder, Abilene

Wagyu Chicken Fried Steak 188
Jean McWilliams, Cross Plains

Desserts

Hundred-Dollar Cake..................... 190
The Texas Cowboys' Christmas Ball, Anson

AA's One-Egg Cake........................ 191
   Jean McWilliams, Cross Plains

Apricot Pie 193
   Hailie Harelik Hubbard, Comanche/
   Brownwood

Apple Pie.................................. 195
   Hailie Harelik Hubbard, Comanche/
   Brownwood

Best Peanut Butter Bars or Balls 197
   Jessica Melson, Abilene

Blueberry Mold............................ 199
   Doris Jackson via Gavin Jackson, Abilene

Bread Pudding with Whiskey Sauce 200
   Dr. Jimmy Harelik, Comanche/Cross Plains

Buttermilk Pie............................. 201
   Margaret Sherrod via Emily Gilmore, Abilene

Chessa's Cheesecake 202
   Ellen Webb via Carol Dromgoole,
   Albany/Abilene

Cherry Crumble Pie 204
   Patricia Pickens, Abilene

Doris's Quick Chocolate Pound Cake..... 208
   Jessica Melson, Abilene

Everybody's Favorite Pecan Pie 209
   Dalya Hight, Aspermont/Old Glory

Foster's Chocolate Cake 211
   Paulette Foster, Cross Plains

Foster's Pie 212
   Paulette Foster, Cross Plains

French Coconut Pie 213
   Roxie Thomas, Cross Plains

Gigi's Sour Cream Pound Cake........... 215
   Whitney Kirkham Henderson,
   Cross Plains

Grown-Up Milk and Cookies............. 218
   Brennan Vineyards, Comanche

Linda's Fresh Carrot Cake................ 219
   Linda Caldwell, Coleman

Oatmeal Caramelitas..................... 222
   Julia Porter Bramblett, Abilene

Paulette's Cookies 223
   Paulette Foster, Cross Plains

Pumpkin Chiffon Pie with
   Gingersnap Crust................... 224
   Elmo Joy Wilson Ferguson, Hamlin, via
   Martha Minter Ferguson

Red Velvet Cake.......................... 225
   Angie Wiley, Abilene

Ruth Bonner's Fresh Coconut Cake 227
   Jean McWilliams, Cross Plains

Strawberry Shortcake 228
   Perini Ranch Steakhouse, Buffalo Gap

Sugar Cookies with Icing................. 230
   Tiffany Prier Lamb, Abilene

Tea Cakes 231
   Maggie Meers, Hamby

Tommy's Spotted Pup
   (Rice and Raisin Pudding) 232
   The Texas Cowboys' Christmas Ball, Anson

Texas Gold 233
   Whitney Kirkham Henderson,
   Cross Plains

Author: Tiffany Harelik 235

Foreword

Finally, a cookbook celebrating the Big Country—a part of Texas that is near and dear to us, because we call it home! We know you will feel right at home with these recipes—a compilation of favorites from the local diners and our neighbors all across the Big Country. The focus of this book is simple: good regional food coupled with exceptional cooks and their stories of the foods that are a part of their families and everyday lives.

As you enjoy *The Big Country Cookbook,* think of West Texas sunsets, great meals you have shared, and all the fond memories you can create around your own table with this book as inspiration.

—Lisa and Tom Perini

Preface

I moved to Taylor County with my parents in the early nineties during my seventh grade year. Coming from the Hill Country where we had big live oak trees, rolling hills, and beautiful lakes, the terrain change to the flatter, red dirt country with mesquite trees and cacti lining the roads was a big change. But I took to it.

One of the first things we did was find a barn where I could continue to ride horses. Inger Svalling's Pegasus Riding Academy at New Colony Farm became a second home to me. I rode every day after school and spent most of the weekend there riding, washing the horses, or cleaning tack. A long trail ride from the barn on Iberis Cemetery Road out to Deutchlander's in Buffalo Gap for a fried catfish lunch with my barn friends was a favorite activity. And looking back, it seems like an awfully long ride on the highway for a bunch of girls who didn't have their keys yet. But we were fearless, and the inherent danger was a main part of the appeal.

I turned sixteen at Joe Allen's with friends from Jim Ned and Wylie, eating sliced brisket and drinking Big Red in the old original building off Treadaway. I went to art camp at the area universities, was sponsored by H. A. Travis Automotive to compete at the scholarship pageant for the Rattlesnake Round-Up over in Sweetwater, played polo at Tommy Taylor's place, went swimming at the Country Club and the State Park in Buffalo Gap, fished in friends' tanks, baled hay, went to football games and rodeos, and soaked up all the experiences the Big Country had to offer. My first job was at Dollar Western Wear on S. 1st, followed by a job doing veterinarian assistant work for Joe Bob Stricklin at Abilene Equine Care. I remember getting donuts at the drive-through, renting movies by Betty Rose's Little Brisket, judging meat with the Future Farmers

photo by Doug Hodel Photography

of America at livestock shows during high school, and making memories with the Wylie High School class of 1999, although I graduated as a junior in 1998.

After high school, I moved away to attend college and graduate school. Eventually, I came back to the Big Country to work for the West Texas Fair and Rodeo as well as the Western Heritage Classic, managing exhibits at the Taylor County Expo Center. The sound of the PRCA announcers welcoming attendees and giving encouragement to the rodeo athletes, the sound of the tractor turning over dirt in the arena, and the taste of a funnel cake on a Ferris wheel ride at sundown brought me back to the joys of my youth. My time working there with Rochelle Johnson and Tony McMillan is where I cut my teeth in event production and remains one of my favorite jobs to date.

I continued to work in large event production for events such as Austin City Limits Music Festival, Lollapalooza Music Festival, Viva Big Bend Music Festival, Trailer Food Tuesdays, Side Project Sundays, and various other clients. While I love working in events, it was in writing books that I really found my stride.

The first book I wrote was an heirloom cookbook project I started in 2007. I wanted to preserve some family histories through recipes and stories to have something to pass down to the next generation. I reached out to everyone on both sides of my family to send me some of their favorite recipes, and I thumbed through all of my mom's cookbooks to type up some of our go-tos. At the completion of that project, I realized that I had a formula down for writing cookbooks and that I really enjoyed the process.

My next eight cookbooks focused on the niche market of food trucks. With a lot of hard work, I self-published and was funded through a Kickstarter project. Eventually I was published through a larger publishing house. With the *Trailer Food Diaries Cookbooks*, I covered Austin, Dallas, and Houston, Texas, as well as Portland, Oregon. I took Renee Casteel Cook under my wing as coauthor for the Columbus, Ohio, edition, which was her first opportunity to be published. Beyond that, I helped curate multiple food truck events and food festivals and began getting offers from TV producers and restaurant owners to consult on turnaround projects. Because I was focused on telling the stories of the entrepreneurs involved as much as sharing their recipes, the theme of the series was "serving up the American Dream, one plate at a time."

I loved writing cookbooks so much, I wanted to take my road trip style formula and go explore my home state. I spent several months in Big Bend country to write *The Big Bend Cookbook* (2015), followed by *The Terlingua Chili Cookbook* (2016).

When I had ten titles under my belt, I was invited back to Abilene to be a featured cookbook author at a fundraiser for the library. Driving through downtown in 2015 was significantly different than it was in the late nineties. McLemore Bass, where I had my first date with Clinton Pickens, had closed, and lots of little stores were revitalizing the area. That weekend, I also taught a little workshop about writing your own cookbook. It was there that I realized I wanted to add the Big Country to my Texas cookbook portfolio, and I approached Abilene Christian University Press with the concept.

I read several community cookbooks from the Big Country while researching this title. Some favorites were just short print runs that are now out of print, while others have a strong national appeal, having sold thousands of copies, such as Tom Perini's. But in my studies, I didn't find anything that represented the broader communities of the area. This fueled my interest in providing a bird's-eye narrative featuring recipes and stories of people from the Big Country.

This cookbook is the combined result of many dinners, hikes, hunts, and sunsets shared with old friends and new ones in the Big Country. My only wish was to have been able to include more people and cover more ground. It has been my honor to write our stories and share the recipes so that future generations might know the people and tables that came before.

photo by Tiffany Harelik

photo by Tiffany Harelik

Introduction

Driving into the Big Country, clusters of cactus pads line the road. Mistletoe hangs from the branches of mesquite trees whose leaves provide little shade. There are cotton fields, hay fields, and peanut fields scattered in patches like a quilt all throughout the Big Country. There are farmers raising cattle for beef, ranchers maintaining the whitetail deer population for hunters, and fishermen pulling bass and catfish out of the area lakes.

Like many parts of Texas, football is a community builder. Football games are a place for the whole family to gather and enjoy their Friday night. Restaurants are stacked full after games with hungry athletes and fans, usually making a late night for all. Basketball, baseball, and track and field are the other main sports. Several youth in the area are also involved with the Future Farmers of America and show their livestock at statewide shows, and the Fellowship of Christian Athletes has a healthy engagement.

Abilene, the seat of Taylor County, is home to the West Texas Fair and Rodeo, a nationally sanctioned rodeo through the Professional Rodeo Cowboy Association. In May, the Taylor County Expo Center also hosts the Western Heritage Classic, a ranch rodeo with unique events such as wild cow milking. There's a large group of equestrians in the area who rope and rodeo in "play days" on the weekends both for fun and for money.

Deep in what many call the Bible Belt, there are more churches per capita in Abilene than in any other area in the state and an estimated two dozen denominations. Although the city was named for Abilene,

photo by Tiffany Harelik

Kansas, some say the name has a biblical heritage as well, referencing Luke 3:1, which mentions Abilene. Hebrew in origin, the name Abilene means land of meadows.

Potosi United Methodist Church is the oldest continually operating church in Taylor County. Founded in 1879, the current building was built in 1905 about a mile north of its original location.

For such a small town, it is noteworthy that there are several universities here, too: Abilene Christian University, Hardin-Simmons University, McMurry University, and Cisco College, a community college. Although area high school graduates end up at all parts of the globe, graduates who pursue college locally choose from these four, as well as nearby Angelo State University in San Angelo or Texas Tech University in Lubbock.

Things have their own pronunciation rules in this part of Texas. If you're driving down Antilley Road in Abilene, you pronounce it ANT-ly. Going to pass through Potosi? That's Puh-TOE-see.

Depending on who you ask, the Big Country is comprised of roughly twenty counties surrounding the Abilene area. For purposes of this book, we include sixteen counties: Stonewall, Haskell, Scurry, Fisher, Jones, Shackelford, Stephens, Mitchell, Nolan, Taylor, Callahan, Eastland, Runnels, Coleman, Brown, and Comanche counties.

ROAD TRIP THROUGH THE BIG COUNTRY

photo by Tiffany Harelik

Big Country

N **W** **S** **E**

Stephens County, home to Breckenridge, Caddo, Eolian, Gunsight, Harpersville, Ivan, Necessity, Reach, Wayland, and La Casa.

Eastland County, home to Eastland, Cisco, Rising Star, Gorman, Ranger, Carbon, Morton Valley, Olden, Romney, Desdemona, and Mangum.

Comanche County, home to Comanche, Beattie, Downing, Gustine, De Leon, Energy, Lamkin, Comyn, Hasse, Hazel Dell, Sidney, Proctor, Newburg, Rucker, Van Dyke, Duster, Promontory, Sipe Springs, Park Springs, and Kentucky.

Brown County, home to Brownwood, Bangs, Early, Blanket, Lake Brownwood, Thunderbird Bay, Brookesmith, Indian Creek, May, Winchell, and Zephyr.

Shackelford County, home to Albany and Moran.

Callahan County, where you'll find Baird, Clyde, Cross Plains, Putnam, Belle Plain, Callahan City, Admiral, Cottonwood, and Eula.

Coleman County, home to Coleman, Novice, Santa Anna, Burkett, Goldsboro, Gouldbusk, Rockwood, Talpa, Valera, and Voss.

Haskell County, home to Haskell, Rule, Irby, Jud, O'Brien, Paint Creek, Rochester, Sagerton, Stamford on the Jones/Haskell county line, and Weinert.

Jones County, home to Anson, Avoca, Nugent, and Stamford. Hawley and Leuders are communities that fall on the Jones/Shackelford county line.

Taylor County, home to Abilene, Tye, Buffalo Gap, Tuscola, Impact, Lawn, Merkel, Trent, Potosi, Caps, Ovalo, View, and Wylie.

Runnels County, home to Ballinger, Winters, Wingate, Norton, Miles, and Rowena.

Stonewall County, home to Aspermont, Old Glory, Peacock, Swenson, and Rath City.

Fisher County, home to Roby and Hamlin, Hobbs, McCaulley, North Roby, Rotan, and Sylvester.

Nolan County, home to Sweetwater, Roscoe, and Blackwell.

Scurry County, home to Snyder, Dermott, Dunn, Fluvanna, Hermleigh, and Ira.

Mitchell County, home to Colorado City, Loraine, Westbrook, and Spade.

The northernmost counties from west to east
are Stonewall and Haskell counties.

Stonewall County, named for Confederate Army General Thomas Jonathan "Stonewall" Jackson, has an estimated population of 1,490. Aspermont is the county seat and was established in 1889. Latin for "rough mountain," Aspermont was likely named for Double Mountain, a prominent pair of flat-topped mountains that divide the Salt Fork and Brazos Rivers, the same location where Comanche Chief Quanah Parker lived with his tribe.

In addition to Aspermont (population approximately 1,000), the unincorporated communities of Old Glory (population approximately 100), Peacock (population approximately 125), Swenson (population approximately 185), and the ghost town of Rath City, which was founded in 1876 but abandoned by 1880, all comprise Stonewall County.

Neighboring **Haskell County** was created in 1858 and named for Tennessee native Charles Ready Haskell who died in battle at Goliad. The county has an estimated population close to 6,000, while the county seat, also named Haskell, has an estimated population of 3,300. The other communities in Haskell county include Irby (population unknown), ghost town Jud, O'Brien (population approximately 100), Paint Creek (population approximately 300), Rochester (population approximately 400), Rule (population approximately 700), Sagerton (population approximately 100), Stamford on the Jones/Haskell county line (population approximately 3,100), and Weinert (population approximately less than 200).

Former Governor of Texas and presidential candidate Rick Perry as well as First Lady Anita Perry are from the Haskell County community Paint Creek.

Although Jud is considered a ghost town, there is still a small farming community in the area. In 1915, they had 31 citizens, but the ruins of an old Baptist church is the only building left standing. Randolph Williams was the pastor in the church's later years. In the summer, JUD FEST takes place with musical performances by local and regional Texas country artists as well as a meat cook-off.

The counties a little to the south and again from west to east are Scurry, Fisher, Jones, Shackelford, and Stephens Counties.

Scurry County was formed in 1876 and has a population close to 17,000. It was named for William Read Scurry, a Confederate Army general. Scurry County spreads across the Llano Estacado, a large mesa flatland area. It was entirely dry until 2006, when the sale of beer and wine was approved in Snyder, the county seat. The sale of liquor by the drink was later approved in 2008.

The Roscoe, Snyder and Pacific Railway Company offers much in the historical development of this area, bringing business to and through Snyder and Fluvanna starting in 1906. The line ran from Roscoe, Texas, to Portales, near the New Mexico state line, to transport freight and passengers with various sections being abandoned at different times. A small section near Roscoe is still in operation today.

Western Texas College (WTC) located in Snyder offers professional development and associate degree programs in applied sciences, including agriculture, art, biology, business administration, chemistry, drama, economics, English, government/history, math, sociology/psychology, speech, and wind energy. You can tune in to KGWB 91.1 FM for broadcasts of WTC athletic games.

WTC offered a room in the early 1970s to launch the Scurry County Museum. The first gallery opened in 1975, and the museum offers rotating exhibits about Scurry County heritage, including things like saddle shop machinery, a large freight elevator, newspaper printing presses, quilts, firearms, and so on. The 1818 Arthouse is an extension of the museum and is located on the square.

In addition to Snyder, Scurry County is comprised of four more unincorporated communities: Dunn (population unknown), Fluvanna (population approximately 200), Hermleigh (population approximately 400), and Ira (population approximately 250).

Fisher County was formed in 1876 and was named for Samuel Rhoads Fisher. Fisher was Secretary of the Navy of the Republic of Texas and was also a signer of the Texas Declaration of Independence. With a population of approximately 3,400, Fisher County is still a dry county, serving and selling no alcohol.

Roby is the county seat and has an approximate population of 650. Widely known for their good luck, the "Roby 42" put Roby on the map in 1996 when forty-two Roby residents pooled their money together and won 46 million dollars in the Texas lottery.

Other communities in Fisher County include Hamlin (population approximately 2,100), Hobbs (population approximately less than 100), McCaulley (population approximately less than 100), ghost town North Roby, Rotan (population approximately 1,600), and Sylvester (population approximately less than 100).

Sammy Baugh, the great quarterback for the Washington Redskins, had a ranch in Rotan, and University of Texas football star Jordan Shipley once attended Rotan High School. Texas Ranger Ramiro "Ray" Martinez, who shot gunman Charles Whitman in the Tower Shooting at the University of Texas in Austin on August 1, 1966, once lived in Rotan, Texas. And actor Tommy Lee Jones made his stage debut at the age of seven as Sneezy in an elementary school pageant of "Snow White and the Seven Dwarves" in Rotan in 1953.

Jones County has a population estimated at 20,200. Initially founded in 1858, Anson was originally named Jones City after the fifth president of the Republic of Texas: Anson Jones. The town of Anson is the county seat, with a population of approximately 2,400.

Anson has hosted the Texas Cowboys' Christmas Ball the weekend before Christmas annually since 1890. The first ball was held at the Star Hotel and hosted by hotel owner M. G. Rhodes. The event died during Prohibition but was brought back to life in 1940 by Leonora Barrett, a local teacher and folklorist. The Christmas Ball's website states: "The tradition of the original dress code is honored. Ladies are required to wear dresses or skirts on the dance floor, split skirts are not allowed. Gentlemen are not allowed to wear hats on the dance floor. Hats and coats may be checked at the door."

Anson Cowboy Christmas Ball

Anson has a "no dancing" law that is lifted only for the three nights of the Christmas Ball. In 1987, an ordinance was passed that allows supervised dancing, which was the inspiration for Ricardo Ainslie's book *No Dancin' in Anson: An American Story of Race and Social Change*. Dr. Paul Carlson's book *Dancin' in Anson* also chronicles the history of the Ball.

Although there may be no dancin' in Anson, it is home to some great singer-songwriters, including country singer Jeannie C. Riley, most famous for her number-one hit "Harper Valley PTA" (1968), who was born in Anson in 1945.

Stamford, on the Jones/Haskell county line, has hosted the Texas Cowboy Reunion since 1930, held every year around the Fourth of July. The gathering was created as a hat tip to Texas cowboy traditions. Will Rogers (1935) and Elvis Presley (1955) both made professional appearances at the reunion. In addition to hosting an amateur rodeo, the reunion showcases a parade, roping, a chuck wagon cook-off, and a Western art show and sale. Stamford is also home to the Stamford Cowboy Country Museum, which offers information on ranching heritage, cowboy art, and antiques.

Jones is one of the few dry counties in Texas. In addition to Anson, Jones County is also home to Avoca (population unknown) and Nugent (population approximately under 50). Additionally, the communities of Hawley (population approximately 600) and Leuders (population approximately 300) are both on the Jones/Shackelford county lines.

Established in 1858, **Shackelford County** was named for Dr. Jack Shackelford. Albany is the county seat, where historic Fort Griffin is located. Residents of Shackelford County have been producing the Fort Griffin Fandangle in Albany since 1938 when locals Robert Nail Jr. and his childhood friend Alice Reynolds created it. The Fandangle is the state's oldest outdoor musical, with a cast of over 250 and over 10,000 in attendance each year. The performance recounts the frontier history of the Fort Griffin military outpost.

The Old Jail Art Center is a community hub that offers exhibitions and special events throughout the year as well as camps and activities aimed at homeschoolers. If visiting Albany, you'll also want to stop in at the Beehive Restaurant, an area favorite for miles around. Opened by brothers Ali and Nariman Esfandiary, Iranian immigrants living in Texas, the Beehive has received recognition from multiple publications, including *Texas Monthly*, who called the Beehive the "best country steakhouse in the state."

In addition to Albany, Shackelford County is home to the community of Moran (population approximately 200). Moran was initially named Hulltown after Swope Hull, the town's first merchant, in 1882. Hulltown was changed to Hicks in 1891 and ultimately to Moran in 1892 after railroad president John J. Moran.

Stephens County was originally named Buchanan County, for President James Buchanan. In 1861 it was renamed Stephens County after the Vice President of the Confederate States of America, Alexander H. Stephens. The population is approximately 9,600. Once home to 50,000 during an oil boom in the 1920s, the county seat of Breckenridge now has a population of approximately 5,800. Breckenridge was also briefly home to western legend John "Doc" Holliday.

Betty E. Hanna's book *Doodle Bugs and Cactus Berries: A Historical Sketch of Stephens County* was written in 1976 and offers more information on the county's history. In addition to Breckenridge, Stephens County is home to the unincorporated communities of Caddo, Eolian, Gunsight, Harpersville, Ivan, Necessity, Reach, and Wayland (populations unknown) as well as the ghost town of La Casa.

A little further south and from west to east again are Mitchell, Nolan, Taylor, Callahan, and Eastland Counties.

Mitchell County has a population of approximately 9,400. It was named for Asa and Eli Mitchell, who were prominent soldiers in the Texas Revolution and early settlers in the area. Colorado City (population approximately 4,100) is the county seat.

The Colorado River enters Mitchell County from the north and flows through the center of the county to the south. A. W. Dunn, the first county treasurer and first storeowner there, was known as the "father" of Colorado City. Colorado City is home to the Heart of West Texas Museum which hosts exhibits that include mammoth fossils, Indian artifacts, railway antiques, WWII heritage, and farming and ranching heritage. Opened in 1959 by Larry Ratliff, the museum is free to the public.

The communities of Loraine (population approximately 600) and Westbrook (population approximately 200) are also part of Mitchell County.

Nolan County was named for Philip Nolan, a frontiersman and horse trader from Ireland. The county has a population of approximately 15,200. The county seat of Sweetwater is world-famous for one of the world's largest Rattlesnake Round-Ups. The local Jaycee chapter started the Round-Up in 1958, and it has been held the second weekend in March annually at Nolan County Coliseum. The town of Sweetwater swells from its normal population of approximately 11,000 to over 40,000 during Rattlesnake Round-Up weekend. The economic impact for the community is estimated at over 5 million dollars for the weekend.

Sweetwater is also home to the National WASP (Women Airforce Service Pilots) WWII Museum. Originally built in 1929, this museum chronicles and honors the first women to fly American military aircraft. The Pioneer City County Museum is another resource that offers historical information on early Nolan County.

Sweetwater was established in 1877 when Billie Knight operated a dugout store for area buffalo hunters. Known for its sweet water amid gypsum streams, the town's name was spelled Sweet Water until 1918 when the spelling changed. Legend has it that the first post office, opened in 1879, was called Blue Goose after local cowboys took down a great blue heron mistakenly thinking it was a variety of goose.

In addition to Sweetwater, Nolan County is comprised of the communities of Roscoe (population approximately 1,400) and Blackwell (population approximately 300).

As previously mentioned, Roscoe used to be part of the Roscoe, Snyder and Pacific Railway in the early 1900s. Now the town hosts the Plowboy Mud Bog twice a year during July and October. Open to anyone with a 4x4 vehicle, the races in the mud benefit Roscoe's Little League Association and pull in a crowd of about a hundred spectators.

Taylor County has a population of approximately 132,000. Established in 1858, the county was named for three brothers who died at the Battle of the Alamo: Edward,

George, and James Taylor. Buffalo Gap, a natural area where bison roamed, was the original county seat in 1878, but in 1883 the county seat was transferred to Abilene.

Abilene, named after Abilene, Kansas, on the end of the Chisolm Trail, was initially organized by a wagon train of families. Captain John T. Lytle moved 3,500 Longhorn cattle from Texas to Nebraska in 1874 on the Great Western Cattle Trail, the most famous of the cattle trails in the area. It ran parallel to the Chisolm Trail and was used to move cattle to more profitable markets in railroad towns and ranches further north. Before the last major cattle drive in 1893, it was estimated that nearly seven million cattle and one million horses had walked the trail from Texas up north.

In 2017, Abilene's population is approximately 117,000. Major destinations include Dyess Air Force Base, the Taylor County Expo Center, the Abilene Zoo, the Grace Museum, Frontier Texas!, the Paramount Theatre, Texas Star Trading Company, the Center for Contemporary Arts, the National Center for Children's Illustrated Literature, the 12th Armored Division Museum, and the Abilene Philharmonic. There are multiple libraries and public parks as well as several historical buildings, including the sixteen-story Wooten hotel built in 1930, the 1946 "Sugar House" (so-named from owner Henry Moreland's career with the Dr. Pepper and 7-Up bottling companies), and the Gothic Revival architecture of Lincoln Junior High School (formerly Abilene High School) originally built in 1923.

Abilene is also home to three major universities: Hardin-Simmons University (founded in 1891), Abilene Christian University (founded in 1906), and McMurry University (founded in 1923), as well as Cisco College, Texas State Technical College, and Texas Tech University Health Sciences Center. There are currently two school districts: Abilene Independent School District and Wylie Independent School District.

Abilene holds the area's largest hospital facility, Hendrick Medical Center, which was originally opened in 1934. Abilene Regional Medical Center and West Texas Medical Center also provide health care to the area.

Abilene hosts several unique events, such as the West Texas Fair and Rodeo (which is held for ten days in September) and the Western Heritage Classic Ranch Rodeo (held during mother's day weekend in May). These events commemorate the cowboy lifestyle with various exhibits and attractions including cowboy poetry, a Western art show, cooking demonstrations, campfire cook-offs, and more. The Crosstown Showdown football game is another highly anticipated annual event between Abilene High and Cooper High held close to Halloween. The West Texas Book Festival, the Abilene Gun and Knife Show, and the Abilene Gem and Mineral Show are other annual attractions. Artwalk is a monthly event held downtown where local museums are free and local artists set up booths to sell items.

Many books have been written about Abilene: *Abilene Stories: From Then to Now* by Glen Dromgoole, Jay Moore, and Joe W. Specht, *Abilene History in Plain Sight* by Jay Moore, *Abilene Landmarks: An Illustrated Tour* by Dr. Donald Frazier, *Lost Abilene: Images of America* by Jack E. North, *Judge Legett of Abilene: A Texas Frontier Profile* by Vernon G. Spence and Rupert Norval Richardson, *Haunted Texas: The Haunted Locations of Abilene and Sweetwater* by Jeffrey Fisher, and *The Abilene Arrangement (Trails to Texas Book 3)* by Posey Marona. Although it is commonly mistaken that Abilene, Texas, inspired the 1963 number one hit song "Abilene" sung by George Hamilton, the songwriter says the song was written about Abilene, Kansas.

In addition to Abilene, Taylor County is comprised of the cities Tuscola (population approximately 700) and Tye (population approximately 1,200), as well as the towns of Buffalo Gap (population approximately 500), Impact (population approximately less than 50), Lawn (population approximately 400), Merkel (population approximately 2,600), and Trent (population approximately 300). Colt McCoy, former quarterback for the University of Texas Longhorns, is from Tuscola, and he went on to play for the Cleveland Browns, as well as quarterback for the Washington Redskins.

Taylor County also includes Potosi (population approximately 1,600) and the unincorporated communities of Caps (population approximately 100), Ovalo (population unknown), View (population approximately 100), and Wylie (population unknown).

Callahan County was named after James Hughes Callahan, a soldier who fought in the Texas Revolution. It has a population of approximately 13,500. Baird is the county seat, with a population of approximately 1,500. The city of Baird was named for Matthew Baird, who owned and directed the Texas & Pacific Railway. Known for its antique shopping opportunities, the Texas Legislature named Baird the Antique Capital of Texas in 1993. The Whistle Stop is a popular breakfast joint nestled in the antique district in the main part of town. The former Callahan County Jail was originally built in the ghost town of Belle Plain. When the county seat was relocated to Baird, the jail was taken apart one brick at a time and rebuilt at its current location.

Callahan County is also comprised of the ghost towns of Belle Plain and Callahan City, as well as the communities of Clyde (population approximately 3,300), Cottonwood (population approximately less than 100), Cross Plains (population approximately 1,000), Eula (population unknown), Admiral (population unknown), and Putnam (population unknown).

Cross Plains was once named "Turkey Creek," after the stream that now crosses the town's Treadaway Park. The community hosts the Robert E. Howard Days and Barbarian Festival on the second weekend of June, which celebrates the life of pulp fiction author Robert E. Howard, who wrote the Conan the Barbarian series and lived in Cross Plains from 1919 until 1936. His former home in Cross Plains is now a museum.

Not too far down the road in Putnam in the same timeframe, Larry L. King was born in 1929. He is a widely recognized author known best for his work *The Best Little Whorehouse in Texas*. The book was later turned into a movie starring Burt Reynolds and Dolly Parton.

Eastland County's county seat is its namesake. Eastland has a population of approximately 18,500. It was named for William Mosby Eastland, a Texas Revolutionary soldier who died as a result of Santa Anna's "black bean lottery." During the Battle of Mier, Santa Anna and commander Huerta offered a compromise whereby instead of killing all of the prisoners, Texas soldiers would be blindfolded and ordered to draw from a bag of white and black beans. The unlucky seventeen men who pulled black beans were given the opportunity to write letters home and were then executed by a firing squad.

Eastland County is also home to Cisco (population approximately 3,800), Gorman (population approximately 1,000), Ranger (population approximately 2,500), Carbon (population approximately 250), and Rising Star (population approximately 800); the unincorporated communities of Morton Valley (population unknown), Olden (population approximately 300), and Romney (population unknown); as well as the ghost towns of Desdemona (population approximately 150) and Mangum (population approximately 10).

Cisco is where Conrad Hilton started his Hilton hotel chain with the purchase of Mobley Hotel in 1919. The original hotel still stands and operates as a museum and community center. Cisco is also known to have the world's largest concrete swimming pool. The Williamson Dam, with a skating rink, zoo, amusement park, and entertainment such as Bob Wills, was built in the 1920s but closed in the 1970s.

Pilot Amelia Earhart landed her Pitcairn Autogyro at Ranger Antique Airfield in 1931.

The first seven families to settle in Rising Star arrived in 1875. The community offered "Star" as their official name when the post office was founded in 1881, but the same town name was already taken. One of the founding family's members, Little Andy Agnew, suggested, "Since we are a rising young community, why don't we just call ourselves 'Rising Star.'"

Originally called Hogtown for its location on Hog Creek, Desdemona was named for the daughter of an area justice of the peace. One of the oldest towns west of the Brazos, Desdemona was originally established in 1857. Producing seven million barrels of oil in 1919, Desdemona became a boomtown, but over the last century became considered a ghost town with less than 200 in population.

A little further south and from west to east again are Runnels, Coleman, Brown, and Comanche Counties.

Runnels County is named for Texas state legislator Hiram Runnels. The county has a population of approximately 10,500.

Ballinger is the county seat and has a population of approximately 3,700. From the 1920s to the 1950s, Ballinger was home to the Ballinger Cats, a minor league baseball team that was affiliated with the Cincinnati Reds and St. Louis Browns.

Runnels County is also home to Miles (population approximately 800), Norton (population approximately 70), Rowena (population approximately 450), Wingate (population approximately 100), and Winters (population approximately 2,500).

The Shed was a BBQ landmark in Wingate owned and operated by local legend Hollis Stephenson and his wife, Betty. Hollis closed the Shed's original location but passed the torch down to his grandson Byron, who operates the family business as a catering unit with his wife and fellow Wylie High School graduate Stacie.

The Z. I. Hale Museum/Rock Hotel was built in Winters as a railroad travelers hotel in 1909. Its modern exhibition includes memorabilia from Hall of Fame baseball legend Roger Hornsby of Winters, musical heritage, antique farm equipment, and more.

Coleman County was founded in 1858 and has a population of about 8,850. The county was named after Robert M. Coleman, a signer of the Texas Declaration of Independence who also fought in the Battle of San Jacinto. Coleman is the county

seat, with a population of about 4,700. The city has hosted an annual Professional Rodeo Cowboy Association (PRCA) sanctioned rodeo in June ever since 1936. Coleman is also home to Owl Drug, a family pharmacy that has been in operation since 1923 where Elvis himself used to frequent. You'll want to order an Owl Burger and grab a soda fountain drink.

Coleman County is also comprised of Novice (population approximately 130), Santa Anna (population approximately 1,050), and the unincorporated communities of Burkett (population unknown), Goldsboro (population approximately 25), Gouldbusk (population unknown), Rockwood (population unknown), Talpa (population approximately 100), Valera (population unknown), and Voss (population approximately 15).

Rockwood is the community closest to the "Heart of Texas," and the twin mesas (Santa Anna's peaks) located in the center of the county are landmarks found on some of the earliest maps of Texas. Named for the Comanche war chief, Santa Anna hosts a World Championship Bison Cook-Off every third weekend in May.

Brown County has a population of about 38,100 and is named for Henry Stevenson Brown, a commander at the Battle of Velasco. Brownwood is the county seat and has a population of approximately 19,200. Camp Bowie, which was a US Army Camp with over 80,000 soldiers during WWII, still operates as a training camp in Brownwood. Lake Brownwood is a popular spot for fishing, camping, and outdoor recreation.

Brown County is also comprised of Bangs (population approximately 1,600), Early (population approximately 2,700), Blanket (population approximately 350), Lake Brownwood (population approximately 1,500), Thunderbird Bay (population approximately 650), and the unincorporated communities of Brookesmith (population unknown), Indian Creek (population unknown), May (population approximately 250), Winchell (population unknown), and Zephyr (population approximately 150).

Comanche County was established in 1856 and was named for the Comanche Native American Indian tribe that resided in the area. It has a population of about 13,900.

Comanche is the county seat, with an approximate population of 4,300. Next to the current county courthouse on the square is the Old Cora Courthouse, one of the oldest wooden courthouses in Texas. The Comanche County Pow-Wow is a fall festival held in City Park that honors the county heritage with arts and crafts, a tractor and classic car show, BBQ cook-off, and more. Situated between the Sabanna and Leon Rivers, Lake Proctor provides fishing and outdoor opportunities for the area.

photo by Tiffany Harelik

Comanche County is also comprised of De Leon (population approximately 2,200), Gustine (population approximately 450), and the unincorporated communities with unknown populations of Beattie, Comyn, Energy, Downing, Duster, Hasse, Lamkin, Newburg, Promontory Park, Rucker, Sidney, Sipe Springs, and Vandyke, as well as Proctor (population approximately 200).

De Leon hosts a Peach and Melon Festival every summer where you can watch tractor pulls, participate in the parade, join the 5K watermelon crawl, and compete for the role of Queen.

Football in the Big Country

Hugh Sandifer

After graduating from Abilene Christian University in 1978, Hugh Sandifer told his wife Brenda he wasn't going to take a coaching job. But in 1979 he accepted an assistant coaching position in the Wylie school district that would be the foundation of his entire coaching career. "I'd always grown up wanting to coach," said Coach Sandifer. "It wasn't like I was telling [Brenda] a story. It just worked out that way. When I took that first job, it was a rural school and community. I really did tell her I'd do it for one year and we'd go somewhere else and I'd get a real job. Now it's year thirty-seven (2016), and believe me I don't get a lot of sympathy when we've had a bad game. She tells me to knock it off or to go get a real job," he said with a smile.

Sandifer, now a coaching legend statewide, has had multiple roles in the Wylie athletic department. He even served as both football and boys' basketball coach from 1986 to 1995. Sandifer has witnessed Wylie outgrow two campuses and rise to be ranked as a 4A school. "We've raised our family here and have enjoyed watching this community grow over the years," said Coach Sandifer.

I asked Coach Sandifer why and how he thought football in the Big Country really brought the community together. "I think in the Big Country, it's still an event," he said. "We don't have the things a lot of the big cities have to go to on Friday night. It's still a social event for schools and towns in the Big Country. Basically when you play a school out in this part, you're playing the whole town. You're not playing the team, you're playing everybody. The way the kids grow up, playing around the field, kids in their jerseys and girls in their cheer outfits—they all dream of being on the field one day."

He has been fortunate to coach at least two NFL stars while coaching at Wylie: Case Keenum (quarterback for the Los Angeles Rams) and Ken Blackman (guard for the Cincinnati Bengals, as well as offseason with the Tampa Bay Buccaneers).

I asked Coach Sandifer what some of his most memorable practices had been. He said, "Practices are the fun part of every team. That's where you spend the most time with your team. I remember one time when a reporter who really had picked on us had come to a game. Someone had picked up a dead rattlesnake from a field and put it in the seat of his car. The guy later started picking us to win. [The reporter] said they had been 'snake bit' earlier in the year but were now picked to win."

Everyone who went to Wylie has such great memories from Hugh and Brenda at pep rallies. I asked Coach Sandifer to talk a little about their inspiration on those. "We still enjoy them," he said. "I think it's pretty cool we have pep rallies. A lot of schools quit doing that. Our band, cheerleaders, and drill team are so good and make school spirit so fun. Brenda and I have always enjoyed the spirit of Wylie, so anything we can do to make it better, we try to do. 'Doing the perfect cheer' from Saturday Night Live skits was totally unexpected by everyone. We had a lot of fun with those. I remember one time I dressed up like Michael Jackson. I don't think I'll ever do that one again," Coach laughs about his experience. "I think it makes high school fun; it's the whole experience. Game days are a big deal. Especially in a coach's life and family. The whole week points to game day. Pep rallies get it going that morning and help everyone stay in the mood all day until game night."

In 2016, Wylie had a little over 1,000 students and was an established 4A high school. Pep rallies are still done in the gym every game day. "A lot of schools just have pep rallies at home games," shared Coach Sandifer, "but we still have them for every game. [In 2016] we played fifteen games and went to the semifinals." That's a lot of school spirit.

Winning the state championship in 2004 has been a career highlight for Coach Sandifer. "We played for three state championships," said Coach. "We lost in 2000 and 2009, but winning in 2004 obviously was big." The 2004 team won it on the last play of the game, kicking a field goal for the win.

"There's a great sense of pride among the community to be the state champion in Texas high school football," shared Coach Sandifer. "To be the champ in your classification is quite the accomplishment. I was so proud of our team for winning it because they had played for all teams past. We were winning and playing for everyone that had ever worn that uniform and played at that school. They wanted to be the first to ever win state. That's what makes high school football so special—we are not just playing the 11 on the field, but for everyone who has gone to that school."

Coach Sandifer said winning state was his most memorable game. "I think anytime when you win a state championship, that's a very memorable game especially in the dramatic style we won by kicking the field goal with four seconds to go."

Coach recalled another memorable game from his earlier coaching days against Ballinger. "We were losing 41 to 13 and came back and won the game 42 to 41. Anytime you have dramatic come-from-behind wins, that's a memorable game."

I asked Coach what turns a team around in those instances you find yourself behind. He said they built their football program on respect. "The respect of your opponent, the game of football, your teammates, and bottom line respecting yourself," said Coach Sandifer. "When you get into critical situations, you have to fall back on respect for yourself and doing your best for your teammates. Coaches can give rah-rahs, but the kids have to perform and that respect we instill in every single one of them."

"That 2004 win has been the only state championship in football we have won. We played for two other state championships and lost. I highly recommend the winning," Coach Sandifer said with a smile. "A lot of people think Wylie is a new school with the growth of Abilene South, but Wylie opened in 1902," he told me. "We had a one hundred-year celebration in 2002, but we've only played football since the 1940s."

I also asked Coach Sandifer about rivalries in the Big Country. "For a long time, [Wylie] had some local rivalries with towns that were of close proximity: Clyde, Merkel, Ballinger," he said. "Through the years, as we have grown and become a larger school, our rivals have changed. Now they are Brownwood, Stephenville, Big Spring, Snyder." Coach Sandifer explained that friendly rivalries exist at the local, district, and even state level.

Football is unmistakably a great tradition, and coaches in the Big Country are critical to this community-centered sporting event. "It's something we take pride in," said Coach Sandifer. "I know everybody talks about the talent base moving to Dallas or Houston, but here it's *team* and that's what we believe in. I think [Big Country coaches] all believe in the same values and we believe in each other. I think it has a lot of tradition and going way back when football was starting in Texas, there was great football in this area. Abilene High winning championships in the 20s and 50s. Albany has had a great tradition, and so on. It's the only place I've ever coached. I've had some opportunities that have humbled me. I don't know—I'll never say I'll never leave, but it's been a great place. Even in college I heard Abilene was a great place to raise a family—so I stayed and had one."

His wife, Brenda, is the director of counseling and testing for Wylie ISD. She worked with Abilene High a few years before transferring her career to Wylie in 1985. Their oldest daughter, Dakota, teaches fourth grade at Wylie, and their younger daughter works in Houston.

Steak in the Big Country

Jason Holloway

Bubba was special.

Unlike the other calves on our farm, Bubba was an orphan. He was bottle-fed as a baby, and he was treated more like a family pet than simply another head in the herd. Bubba was always anxious for his next bottle, so there was no real reason to keep him fenced—he would hang around the house of his own volition, waiting to be fed. My siblings and I would play games of football with Bubba in the backyard; he would chase and tackle whoever held the ball. My family likes to say Bubba went to college, because he spent some time as a teaching tool at Abilene Christian University. Students enrolled in the school's agriculture program would judge Bubba against other steers his age, learning to inspect and identify the qualities that make up a better beef bovine. And it was in this way that Bubba was no different than any of the other cattle on our farm: Bubba was delicious.

There's no shortage of cattle in the Big Country; our counties hold more cows than people—from lawn-ornament longhorns to prize-winning show steers. Even as I'm writing this, a young man from Anson just won Grand Champion Steer at the Fort Worth Livestock Show. It's the same show where my uncle, Wilburn Holloway, won Grand Champion back in 1960. You can still see that steer, stuffed and mounted as a trophy, hanging on the wall of Cattlemen's Steak House at the Fort Worth Stockyards. His Hereford head is there to greet you as you walk in the door—suspended next to a photo of my uncle and grandfather. Despite the Holloway connection, my family and I never took a trip to dine in that steak house. My parents wouldn't be caught dead paying Cattlemen's prices for a steak dinner. And really, why should they? Even in slim years on the farm, when drought conditions would dry up the family business (and force us kids to forfeit any hope of big Christmas gifts), there was one delicacy in constant supply: steak.

I say "delicacy," but the idea of steak as something super special is still rather foreign to me. More often than not, our family dinners and suppers were dominated by steak. My mother kept a cupboard full of recipe books, but there was seldom reason to crack one open. Sunday . . . steak. Monday . . . steak. Tuesday . . . you get the idea. I remember taking trips to Grandma's house (mom's side of the family), and getting super excited about the exceptional dinner I knew would be awaiting me. Grandma's signature dish? Ramen noodles. They don't serve Top Ramen at Cattlemen's Steak House; there wouldn't be enough customers willing to pay 45 dollars for a 12-ounce portion.

In the Big Country, my perception of steak as an everyday food is not entirely unique. One of my best childhood friends also grew up around cattle. After moving to Dallas/Fort Worth for college, he would find it strange when fellow students would suggest a steak dinner for special occasions. "Why in the world would we want to get steak?" he would ask. "Isn't there a chicken place that's close by?" I was well into my own college tenure before I discovered the concept of steak temperature. Blue, rare, medium, well done. On the farm, there was only one meat temperature: cooked.

I was well into my twenties before learning the differences in steak cuts. New York, tenderloin, and rib eye were not terms of my youth. Steak was simply steak, and there was only one way to prepare it: chicken fried. To this day, I love chicken fried steak. Paired with mashed potatoes and gravy, it's a meal one can buy *anywhere* in the Big Country—from old-time diners to Mexican restaurants. But it's not a universal meal. My wife and I moved to Boston for work in 2013. A few weeks into our New England residency, we visited a cute greasy spoon up the road from the house we were renting. We walked in, sat down, and (without glancing at the menu) placed our order: chicken fried steak. The waitress looked confused: "Chicken fried steak? What's that?" My wife and I soon left Boston, never to return.

But back to Bubba . . .

Bubba's twice-daily bottle-feeding regimen was just one of multiple chores on our farm; his breakfast bottle was an early-morning chore—the kind that had to be done prior to catching the bus to school. Life is similar for most kids growing up on Big Country farms: chores before school, go to school, chores after school, homework, a few more chores, and bed. That's a Monday. Wake up Tuesday and do it all again. Feed hay to the cattle, because there's not enough rain to grow grass. Plow the fields, because there is enough rain to grow weeds. Move cattle from pasture to pasture, because there's not enough rain to keep tanks (rancher-slang for "ponds") full of water. Wait for a decent rain, so you're able to plant the fields with wheat, milo, or cotton. Vaccinate the cattle, so they won't fall to disease. Tag the calves' ears with a unique number, so they can be easily identified. Cull the older calves from their moms, so they may be sent to auction. Harvest whatever wheat, milo, or cotton you managed to grow. (If only we had some more rain.) Have a conversation with neighboring farmers about the lack of rain. Maintain the heavy equipment—tractors, combines, plows, trailers—it takes to operate a farm and ranch.

That's a Tuesday.

For kids on a farm, school is nothing short of a vacation from work. My siblings and I loved going to school, and we dreaded coming home—knowing our father would most likely greet us at the door with his standard salutation: "Get your work clothes on." It didn't take us long to discover that extracurricular activities could serve as a day-pass from hard labor. My brothers played football, because two-a-day practices offered twice-a-day reprieve from the farm. My sister played basketball, because away games were consistently contested away from the farm. I was involved in theater, speech, UIL academics, and band. You could say I acted, spoke, thought, and played my way away from the farm. Summer vacations were the absolute worst, because the work days went without interruption—sunrise to sunset. Sometimes longer. I spent many fifteen-hour days in the seat of a tractor with no entertainment other than an AM radio and my own imagination. I would imagine having the power to teleport away from the farm. (No joke.) By the time I graduated high school, I had been a Holloway Farms employee for eighteen years.

And that employment was a gift. I entered college and the private sector with a work ethic and sense of responsibility uncommon to many in my generation. I put in long hours for my company, because even my busiest days at the office never feel too taxing. I've traded my old work clothes—worn out jeans, steel-toed boots, and torn up T-shirts—for suits, dress shirts, and polished shoes; but the values I bring daily to the office are still the ones born on a Big Country wheat and cattle farm.

These days, corporations are swallowing many American family farms—replacing tradition and time-tested practices with scientific breakthroughs and time-saving efficiencies. Food for your table is still grown from the fields, but sons and daughters are being swapped for hourly employees. Chemical compounds mean more bounty in less time. Selective breeding and cloning (yes, it's already happening) mean more beef from a single steer. Better practices and bigger operations designed to drive down the cost of tomorrow's dinner. Some call this progress; some would call it evolution. I would say the future of farming is bright, but sterile. The character and beating heart of a true family farm will soon be the stuff of nostalgia. Soon. But right now, the character still remains. The heart still beats. Those old-fashioned family farms continue to serve as the pulse of the Big Country.

Growing Food in the Big Country

Mike Hardwick

Born in May, Texas, Mike Hardwick was part of May's very first six-man football team. "We played Brookesmith, Sidney, Potsville, and Gustine," he recalled. He was one of ten students in the graduating class of 1969.

In 1869, his great-grandfather, Hut Buzbee, settled the land Mike still owns and farms. "My great-grandparents came from Frankfurt on the Main in Germany," Mike shared. "They came through Ellis Island and came to May, Texas, from Chicago, Illinois, in 1919. The oil boom hit and they had a well that covered 160 acres with oil. They moved to Pioneer in a tent camp to keep exploring the potential oil opportunities with thirty thousand other people. There are still remnants of the concrete from those early settlements in Pioneer today."

Mike opened his first fruit and vegetable store in Rising Star in 1997, laying the foundation for other stores throughout the Big Country. The second location was built in Mineral Wells, followed by the Cross Plains and Eastland locations. He employees a dozen people at any given time, and at his busiest held over two dozen staff.

photo by Tiffany Harelik

"We were growing three hundred to four hundred acres of watermelons commercially," Mike shared, "before we started to do retail only. We now take all our products from start to finish on a forty-acre truck garden." His diverse operation grows everything they sell. He has a seven-acre peach orchard, thirty acres of cantaloupes and watermelons, an acre of okra, and large patches of tomatoes, cucumbers, squash, black-eyed peas, onions, potatoes, and more.

"We used to grow fifteen hundred acres of peanuts in Brown, Eastland, and Comanche Counties, too," said Mike, who was part of the Southwest Peanut Growers Association.

I worked for Mike and Janna Hardwick for several months at their Rising Star location in 2006. I asked Mike what people could do at home to maintain a good garden for personal consumption. He taught me that there are three things that make plants grow: sun, water, and nutrients. While most gardeners are aware to keep their soil supplied with nitrogen, phosphorus, and potassium, we need to be aware that plants also need trace elements and minerals that are often too expensive to maintain. The solution? Don't overwork the land with irrigation and too quick of a turnaround on vegetable plots. Give the soil a chance to rebuild its nutrients naturally and organically.

RECITES

from Granny
(Margaret
Sherrod) Buttermilk Pie

1 (9 inch) unbaked pie shell

1/2 cup butter   3 eggs, beaten
1 1/2 cup sugar   1 cup buttermilk
3 Tablespoon flour

Melt butter and let cool. Add sugar and
mix well. Add flour and eggs; beat
well. Stir in buttermilk. Pour into
unbake pie shell. Bake at 350° for
45-50 minutes. Cool on wire rack before
serving.

BEVERAGES

AA's Egg Nog
Ada Cutbirth, Cross Plains, via Jane Cutbirth Bonner

Big Country Sunset Margaritas
Katie Browning, Abilene

Easy Wassail
Connie Kirkham, Cross Plains

Rosealea Bonner's Shower Punch
Jean McWilliams, Cross Plains

Sherbet Punch
Connie Kirkham, Cross Plains

Strawberry, Cherry Basil Lemonade
Tiffany Harelik, Buffalo Gap/Cross Plains

Texas Milk Punch
Elizabeth Wagstaff, Abilene

The Mill Wineritas
Bridget McDowell, Aspermont/Abilene

AA's Egg Nog

Jane Bonner, Cross Plains

This was Ada Cutbirth's recipe; she was known as AA. It makes approximately 1 gallon. If you'd like to make less, use this ratio: 1 tablespoon whiskey: 1 tablespoon sugar: 1 egg. About one egg per serving is a good rule of thumb.

    8 eggs, separated
    8 tablespoons whiskey
    8 tablespoons sugar
    pinch salt
    1 pint whipped cream

Beat all egg yolks together. Add whiskey one tablespoon at a time and beat. Add sugar and beat. Beat 1 pint whipped cream separately and put in the fridge. Beat egg whites separately until stiff. Fold whipped cream into egg yolk mixture. Fold in beaten egg whites last.

Bear Branch

The Cutbirth Ranch is one of the oldest continuously run ranches in Callahan County. In 1877, Jasper B. Cutbirth drove his herd of white faced Hereford cattle onto what would become the Cutbirth Ranch. The Cutbirth family has made Cross Plains home for over one hundred years. Sisters Jean McWilliams and Jane Bonner still live in Cross Plains. Jane operates Bear Branch, a hunting ranch that specializes in whitetail deer and turkey hunting, while Jean and her husband manage the UF, a local beef cattle ranch. Ada, or AA as Jane and Jean called her, had many ranch stories from early pioneer days including how *her* mother would hide the children in the cellar or attic when the "friendly Indian" would come by the ranch for food or water.

"Daddy Fred ran the ranch and marketed the cattle," Jean shared. About the UF brand, she said: "In the early 1900s before they made brands together, the brand letters were all freehand and cut in single letters: C, U, T. Some of his nieces and nephews said UF stood for 'Uncle Fred,' but I think he just took the letters he had and made it into a UF."

Jane told me the story of their calf Strawberry. "We saw [Daddy Fred] load her onto the same trailer where all the calves go to cow heaven, and we threw a fit on the porch, crying and screaming. So he went and unloaded her and let us raise her." Strawberry would go on to produce several calves, and the girls got to keep the money earned from each sale.

photo by Tiffany Harelik

Jane also raised miniature horses at Bear Branch for several years. Her stallion, Stonehenge Painted Feather, or Feather as she calls him, produced multiple world champions through the American Miniature Horse Association. Feather and Jane's last three mares are now retired on a wedding farm in Arkansas.

Jane's family continues to develop wildlife management programs on their land. "We offer white tail, Rio Grande turkey, and mourning dove hunts," she shared. "It's a full package deal. We cook, [my son] Trey guides all the hunts, and we offer them room at the bunk house."

Jean and Joe McWilliams have been developing beef for public consumption at the UF Ranch. Starting with the family's herd of white faced Herefords, they transitioned to Angus, and now produce Wagyu. "2012 was the first year we were introduced to Wagyu," shares Jean. "We bought some from a breeder to eat, and we liked it. So we have incorporated them into our program. We decided we liked the half bloods better until we had the three-quarter bloods," she laughs. They have about one hundred registered head of cattle at any given time. "The Wagyu is more tender and tastes better than what we were producing before," Jean shared. "We want to sell the best meat we can, so we have been transitioning over."

Joe and Jean are the sixth generation that have been breeding cattle for public consumption.

photo by Tiffany Harelik

Big Country Sunset Margaritas

Katie Browning, Abilene

photo by Kristina Wolter

The blood orange juice gives a beautiful, vibrant color and taste to these margaritas.

    ⅔ cup fresh blood orange juice
    3 tablespoons fresh lime juice
    3 tablespoons Cointreau
    6 tablespoons blue agave tequila (or any high-quality clear tequila)

Dip rims of two glasses in blood orange juice and then lightly coat the rims by dipping them in a mixture of sugar and salt.

Mix in a cocktail shaker with ice and strain and pour over ice. Serves 2. Quantities can be multiplied for large batches.

Easy Wassail

Connie Kirkham, Cross Plains

"This is delicious and a quick holiday drink in a hurry." —Connie Kirkham

    1 package cinnamon Red Hots
    1 large apple juice

Put juice in percolator and Red Hots in the basket. Perk as you would coffee.

Rosealea Bonner's Shower Punch

Jean McWilliams, Cross Plains

"This makes about fifty glasses of punch if served in punch cups. This recipe has been passed around from the early '70s. It can go most any color Jell-O used and all taste alike. The watermelon was a little different. Frozen punch will be darker than after you add the ginger ale." —Jean McWilliams

Boil to dissolve sugar:

    4 cups water
    3 cups sugar

Add and bring to boil:

    4 cups water
    2 packages Jell-O (any flavor depending on the color desired)

Add:

    1 tall can pineapple juice
    1 large lemonade (pink for color)
    ½ ounce almond extract

Freeze in an ice cream bucket or two-gallon baggies.

To serve:

Sliver in thin, narrow pieces for a slushy punch.

After all is slivered, pour 3 quarts of ginger ale over and stir.

Sherbet Punch

Connie Kirkham, Cross Plains

photo by Mary Lancaster

This is an easy punch that is great for any gathering or celebration.

½ gallon sherbet of your choice (strawberry, orange, lime)
1 3-liter lemon-lime soda or ginger ale

Empty sherbet in a punch bowl. Add lemon-lime soda or ginger ale. Mix and serve cold.

Strawberry Cherry Basil Lemonade

Tiffany Harelik, Buffalo Gap/Cross Plains

We served the "Strawberry Basil Balsamic Lemonade" recipe from Pompeii food truck as featured in *Trailer Food Diaries Cookbook* (Dallas/Fort Worth edition) at a library fundraiser luncheon in Abilene (2015). It went over so well that I decided to put my personal touch on it and add it to this cookbook. This will make one pitcher and can easily be adjusted for different tastes. You can add other fruits like frozen blueberries or raspberries.

    11-pound clamshell container fresh strawberries from Childress Farm in Cottonwood
    8–12 fresh cherries, pits removed
    12–15 lemon basil leaves (fresh)
    juice of 8–10 lemons, deseeded
    ¾ cup–1 cup sugar or more to taste
    ¼ cup brown sugar
    dash balsamic glaze, optional

Remove stems from strawberries. Mash strawberries, cherries, and basil with a mortar and pestle. Add ¾ cup to 1 cup white sugar and allow to sit in a bowl about an hour to allow fruit to macerate. Strain the fruit mash with a cheesecloth or other straining device to extract the juices into a pitcher.

Add fresh lemon juice, brown sugar, and balsamic glaze to taste. You can add part of the fruit pulp or some whole strawberries and cherries or basil leaves to brighten the pitcher or garnish each glass. To save time, you can buy lemonade and just add the cherries, strawberries, basil, and balsamic according to taste.

Texas Milk Punch

Elizabeth Wagstaff, Abilene

"Texas Wagstaff, my husband's grandmother, brought this family tradition to Abilene from her home town of Bryan. She oversaw the preparation of this magic elixir on Christmas Day, which is guaranteed to fortify and restore the weariest of Santa's helpers." —Elizabeth Wagstaff

½ cup pure cane sugar
1 cup Southern Comfort whiskey (Texas used extra ⅓ cup)
4 cups cold whole milk
nutmeg
crushed ice

In a pitcher, whisk and dissolve the sugar in the Southern Comfort, then stir in the milk. Pour over crushed ice, and top with fresh nutmeg. Sip and savor.

The Mill Wineritas

The Mill Winery, with Bridget McDowell, Aspermont/Abilene

photo by Tiffany Harelik

The wineritas are some of the Mill Winery's customers' favorites. Bridget says you can use any three bottles of white wine you like to help adjust the taste to your preference.

2 12-ounce cans frozen limeade
1 liter 7Up (or water if you don't like carbonation)
1 bottle chardonnay
2 bottles moscato (or other sweet wine)

Mix, chill, and serve over ice with salted rim and lime wedge.

The Mill

Mother-daughter business partners Bridget McDowell and Mindy Howard purchased the Mill in October of 2013. Bridget's husband, Gerry, was the general contractor and began renovating the property to transform it into a wine bar and event center. They opened in 2014.

"The sangria is our best seller," shared Bridget, "followed by our house wine." Because they have a beer and wine license, they are not permitted to manufacture their own beer and wine, but they do label their products to sell (non-exclusively).

"We see a lot of weddings, receptions, and proposals here," Bridget told me. There's also a cigar bar. "That's Gerry's doing," Bridget said with a grin, "and it does surprisingly well."

Originally from Aspermont, Bridget graduated with forty-two other students in 1982. She met her husband Gerry, who was a class ahead of her, at Aspermont during high school. They were married in Peacock, Texas, in 1983. Their three daughters, Mindy, Misty, and Mitzy, all live and work in the Big Country.

photo by Tiffany Harelik

BREAKFASTS

Betty Jim's Cheese Blintzes
Betty Jim Parks Harelik, Comanche, via Tiffany Harelik

Breakfast Braid
Connie Kirkham, Cross Plains

Breakfast Bundt Cake
Roxie Thomas, Cross Plains

Breakfast Cups
Connie Kirkham, Cross Plains

Christmas Morning Coffee Cake
Martha Minter Ferguson, Abilene

Cinnamon Waffles
Connie Kirkham, Cross Plains

Connie's Breakfast Casserole
Connie Kirkham, Cross Plains

Mer's Sausage Egg Casserole
Jessica Melson, Abilene

Poppy Seed Sausage Rolls
Melanie Brown, Abilene

Tomato Florentine Quiche
Connie Kirkham, Cross Plains

Betty Jim's Cheese Blintzes

Betty Jim Parks Harelik, Comanche, via Tiffany Harelik

"My Dad's mom used to make these yummy blintzes. I found this recipe among my grandmother's recipes, and it's the one I use. This recipe yields 6 servings."
—Tiffany Harelik

Blintze batter:

> 1 cup flour
> ½ teaspoon salt
> 4 eggs
> 1 cup milk (can substitute with water)
> butter

Sift together flour and salt. Beat eggs; add liquid; beat again. Gradually add flour to eggs, stirring constantly to make a thin, smooth batter.

Lightly grease a six-inch skillet with butter. Place skillet over a moderately high flame. Fill a cup with batter. Pour about ½ cup of batter into skillet. As soon as batter sticks to the skillet, pour excess back into cup. Fry until blintze begins to "blister" and edges curl away from skillet; top of blintze may be slightly moist.

Turn out onto a plate, fried side up. Be sure and keep skillet greased after about every third blintze. Then place 1 tablespoon filling in the center of each blintze (on the brown side). Raise the bottom flap of dough to cover the filling, then overlap the other flaps of dough. Fry in a liberal amount of butter until lightly browned on both sides. Serve hot with applesauce or sour cream.

Cheese filling:

> 1 pound cottage cheese
> 1 egg yolk
> 1 tablespoon melted butter
> 1 tablespoon sugar
> pinch salt
> ⅓ teaspoon cinnamon, optional

Mix together.

Blueberry filling:

  2 cups blueberries
  2 tablespoons sugar
  2 tablespoons flour

Sprinkle blueberries with sugar and flour.

Apple filling:

  2 cups chopped apples
  2 egg whites
  ½ cup chopped nuts
  sugar and cinnamon to taste

Combine all ingredients.

Breakfast Braid

Connie Kirkham, Cross Plains

photo by Suzanna Cole

This breakfast meal is as beautiful as it is versatile.

    1 tablespoon olive oil
    1 small onion, diced
    ½ red bell pepper, large dice
    ½ yellow bell pepper, large dice
    ¼ green bell pepper, large dice
    1 teaspoon fresh rosemary, chopped, plus a little extra for garnish
    salt and pepper to taste
    6 eggs
    1 cup shredded cheese, plus extra for topping
    2 packages crescent rolls
    2–3 tablespoons melted butter

Preheat oven to 350°. Heat oil in a large nonstick skillet. Add onions, followed by bell peppers, and sauté 2 to 3 minutes. As vegetables soften, whisk eggs with rosemary, salt, and pepper in a bowl. Add to veggies and cook, approximately 3 to 5 minutes. Add 1 cup shredded cheese and stir into egg mixture.

Unroll crescent rolls and separate the triangles. Place the short edges of two triangles together, with the long tips pointing opposite directions, and place on a baking sheet (use a silicone mat if available). Place the next pair of triangles with the tips at the long side base of the previous ones, so it resembles a Christmas tree. Repeat

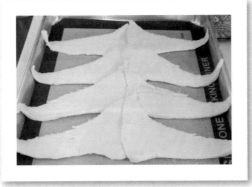

photo by Suzanna Cole

with remaining crescent roll dough; you can make one long one if you have a large enough pan or two medium-sized ones. (Alternately, unroll one tube of crescent roll dough into one large rectangle. Pinch all seams together. Along one long side, make cuts about two inches apart about a third of the way through; repeat on opposite side.)

photo by Suzanna Cole

Fill the center of the rolls with the egg mixture. Bring the points over to make a braid. Brush melted butter on the top and sprinkle cheese plus a small amount of rosemary. Bake at 350° until the dough is cooked and turns light brown, about 15 minutes. Cool and serve.

photo by Suzanna Cole

Breakfast Bundt Cake

Roxie Thomas, Cross Plains

"This cake travels well! Our family traditionally travels to Port Aransas for the Fourth of July, and I always bake this recipe to take along. Even with haphazard packing, it holds up and is moist and delicious." —Roxie Thomas

    1 package yellow cake mix
    1 package instant vanilla pudding
    4 eggs
    ¾ cup water
    ¾ cup vegetable oil
    2 teaspoons vanilla extract
    ¼ cup brown sugar
    2 teaspoons cinnamon

Preheat oven to 350°. Grease and flour a round Bundt pan.

In a small bowl, mix cinnamon and brown sugar. Set aside. Combine cake mix and pudding mix. Add oil and water and mix well. Add eggs one at a time, mixing well after each egg. Beat 6 to 8 minutes on high. Add vanilla.

Pour a third of the cake batter into the pan and sprinkle with cinnamon mixture. Top with remaining batter. Bake for about 50 minutes or until toothpick comes out clean. Can glaze with a mixture of 1 cup powdered sugar, 3 tablespoons milk, and 1 teaspoon vanilla.

Breakfast Cups

Connie Kirkham, Cross Plains

"These are really neat for Easter, as the hash browns make a nest." —Connie Kirkham

    Frozen hash browns, as much as needed
    1 red bell pepper, diced
    ½ onion, diced
    1 clove garlic, minced
    1 meat of choice (bacon, ham, sausage)
    12 eggs (or one egg per cup)
    shredded cheese, to top

Preheat oven to 350°. Grease a twelve-cup muffin tin. Place slightly thawed out hash browns in the cups to make a nest for the filling.

Sauté bell pepper with onion, garlic, and meat of choice. Put one tablespoon of the meat mixture on top of the hash browns in each cup.

Whip one egg per cup. Pour on top of meat mixture. Top with shredded cheese. Bake at 350° for 10 to 15 minutes until the egg is done.

Christmas Morning Coffee Cake

Martha Minter Ferguson, Abilene

"Make this in a foil Christmas tree-shaped pan for gift giving to special friends!"
—Martha Minter Ferguson

Batter:

1½ cups all-purpose flour
2 teaspoons baking powder
1 cup sugar
½ cup butter
2 eggs, separated
pinch salt
½ cup whole milk

Preheat oven to 300°. Sift together the flour and baking powder. Cream butter and sugar together; add salt and egg yolks. Alternate adding flour and milk to the butter mixture, ending with flour.

Beat the egg whites until stiff. Fold into batter.

Filling:

2 tablespoons butter
1 cup brown sugar
1 cup chopped pecans
1 tablespoon cinnamon

Melt butter; add sugar, cinnamon, and pecans. Mix well.

In a greased and floured Bundt pan, alternate batter and filling, letting the filling be the last (top) layer. Bake on 300° for 10 minutes. Raise the oven temperature to 350° and bake 25 more minutes, or until the cake tests "done" by inserting a toothpick and making sure the toothpick comes out dry. Leave in the pan to cool before serving.

Cinnamon Waffles

Connie Kirkham, Cross Plains

photo by Kristina Wolter

"Kids love these!" Connie says.

1 package Pillsbury cinnamon rolls

waffle iron

Place a roll in each quarter of a waffle iron sprayed with Pam. Remove waffle and pour the icing that comes with the cinnamon rolls over the waffles while they are still warm.

photo by Kristina Wolter

Connie's Breakfast Casserole

Connie Kirkham, Cross Plains

1 small bell pepper, chopped

1 small onion, chopped

1–2 pounds sausage, bacon, or ham

4 slices day-old bread (whole wheat)

18 eggs, whipped

2 cups cheddar cheese, shredded and divided

1 cup sour cream

1 teaspoon dried rosemary or dried basil (optional)

salt to taste

pepper to taste

garlic salt to taste

Preheat oven to 350°. Sauté bell pepper, onion, and meat together. Add 1 tablespoon of olive oil if you are using ham. If you're using ham or bacon, chop it after cooking. Drain any fat.

Break bread in small pieces and place in the bottom of a greased 9x13 pan. Pour whipped eggs in an oiled skillet to scramble until soft. Add eggs to meat and vegetable mix. Fold in 1 cup cheese, sour cream, and herbs if using.

Add salt, pepper, and garlic salt to taste. Pour mixture over the bread, then top with 1 cup cheese. Bake at 350° for 20 minutes.

Mer's Sausage Egg Casserole

Jessica Melson, Abilene

"This is from my best friend Meredith and always goes fast. It's one of my most requested recipes." —Jessica Melson

 1 pound sausage, browned
 3 slices white bread, cubed
 6 eggs
 2 cups milk
 1 teaspoon salt
 1 teaspoon dry mustard
 1 cup Velveeta, cubed
 1 cup cornflakes
 ½ cup butter, melted

Butter or spray a 9x13 baking dish. Place cubed bread in pan. Add sausage and cubed Velveeta over bread. Beat eggs, milk, mustard, and salt together in a bowl, and pour evenly over the bread, sausage, and cheese. Cover and refrigerate overnight.

Bake 35 minutes at 350°. Remove from the oven to spread cornflakes over top and drizzle butter over cornflakes. Bake 10 more minutes. Let stand 15 minutes before serving.

photo by Tiffany Harelik

Poppy Seed Sausage Rolls

Melanie Brown, Abilene

photo by Kristina Wolter

This recipe tastes as great as it looks. Simple ingredients make it easy to put together on short notice to have something unique to serve.

1 pound venison sausage
8 ounces cream cheese
2 cans crescent rolls
1 egg white
poppy seeds

Preheat oven to 350°. Brown sausage; drain very well. Return the sausage to the warm skillet and mix in the cream cheese thoroughly. Shape crescent dough into two rectangles. Form the sausage and cheese mixture into two logs and place on rectangles. Roll up dough over the logs and set seam-side down on a baking sheet.

Brush the tops with egg white and sprinkle with poppy seeds. Bake at 350° for 20 minutes. Allow to cool. Slice and serve warm.

Melanie Brown

Born and raised in Abilene, Melanie Brown is a third-generation Abilenian. There were 612 in her graduating class from Cooper High School in 1975, where she loved to play tennis. Melanie left the Big Country for a few years to attend college and work in Dallas, and she ultimately returned to Abilene to raise her two children.

"My grandparents came here from Oklahoma for oil business and were very successful," shared Melanie. "Growing up, my mother cooked every night, but it was mainly from cans and packages. She was a 'convenience food cook.' I thought it was fine until as an adult I realized what real cooking was. It was actually due to a few friends of mine that are good cooks that I learned to appreciate real food and actual cooking, so I really began learning. And I try to learn from my husband who is a natural cook—and a great one!"

Melanie also shared that a Briarstone turkey and dressing was the mainstay at holidays in her house. She owned a gift shop for ten years and is now mainly a homemaker and mom.

Tomato Florentine Quiche

Connie Kirkham, Cross Plains

This garden-fresh breakfast dish is a great way to start the day.

1 10-ounce package frozen spinach, thawed
1 14½-ounce can petite diced tomatoes, drained
2 tablespoons Italian seasoned breadcrumbs
3 large eggs
1 cup half and half
4 bacon slices, cooked and crumbled
½ cup sharp cheddar cheese, shredded
½ cup mozzarella cheese, shredded
1 teaspoon pesto seasoning or dried basil
¼ teaspoon ground red pepper
1 unbaked, frozen pie pastry crust

Drain spinach and press dry with paper towels. Toss diced tomatoes with breadcrumbs.

Stir together eggs, half and half, bacon, spinach, and remaining ingredients. Fold in the tomato mixture.

Pour into frozen pastry crust and place on baking sheet. Bake at 350° for 50 minutes. Remove from oven and let stand 20 minutes before serving.

BREADS

Chuck Wagon Sourdough Biscuits
Cowboy Museum, Stamford, via Sandra Rhea

Granny's Banana Nut Bread
Connie Kirkham, Cross Plains

Healthy, Yummy Muffins
Kaye Price-Hawkins, Abilene

Jimmy's Thanksgiving Rolls
Dr. Jimmy Harelik, Comanche/Cross Plains

Mexican Corn Bread
Connie Kirkham, Cross Plains

Navajo Fry Bread
Lola Molina, Buffalo Gap

Potato Refrigerator Rolls
Willie May Rider, Early

Refrigerator Rolls
Mary Frances Morgan, De Leon, via Kay Harelik Morgan

Chuck Wagon Sourdough Biscuits

Cowboy Museum, Stamford, via Sandra Rhea

"Please note this is an old chuck wagon recipe, to cook in the coals of a campfire, so no temperature is given for baking, also no time is indicated on the sourdough starter. It is done when it's 'done rising.'" —Sandra Rhea

Biscuits:

1 cup sourdough starter

3–4 cups flour

1 teaspoon salt

1 teaspoon sugar

1 teaspoon baking soda

1 tablespoon shortening, plus melted shortening for baking

Place flour in a bowl and add the sourdough starter. Stir in the salt, baking soda, sugar, and shortening. Dough should begin to form. Add flour until the dough is firm. Pinch off some dough, form a ball, and roll it in melted shortening. Place the biscuits in a Dutch oven. Allow the biscuits to rise for about 20 minutes. Then bake until they're done, about 30 minutes.

Sourdough starter:

In order to make sourdough, you'll need some sourdough starter. Here's how to make it.

2–3 potatoes

2 cups flour

1 tablespoon sugar

First, you need to make your potato water by cutting up a couple of medium-sized potatoes into cubes and boiling them in 3 cups of water until the potatoes are tender. Measure two cups of the potato water, and mix it with flour and sugar into a paste. Set the mixture in a warm place to rise. It should double its original size after it's done rising.

Granny's Banana Nut Bread

Connie Kirkham, Cross Plains

photo by Juilet Mossman

This is a great way to use up your ripe bananas.

- 3 cups sugar
- 1 cup shortening
- 4 eggs
- 2 teaspoons vanilla
- ½ cup buttermilk
- 2 teaspoons baking soda
- 4 cups flour
- 3 ripe bananas, mashed
- 1 cup walnuts or pecans

Cream shortening and sugar. Add eggs one at a time and mix well. Add vanilla and blend. Combine buttermilk and baking soda. Add alternately with flour, starting and ending with flour. Add mashed bananas and blend.

Bake in a well-greased and floured tube pan or two loaf pans. Bake at 300° until a toothpick inserted comes out clean. Try 2 hours for a tube pan and 1½ hours for loaves. Don't rush baking.

Healthy, Yummy Muffins

Kaye Price-Hawkins, Abilene

"My mother calls these 'Blow-Out Muffins.'" —Kaye Price-Hawkins. This recipe yields approximately three dozen muffins. Original recipe by Lottie Novak, modified by Joe Hawkins and Kaye Price-Hawkins.

Mix these ingredients until smooth in large mixing bowl.

photo by Crystal Johnson

¾ cup canola oil
3 eggs
½ cup sugar
¾ cup brown sugar
1 cup cooking Splenda
1 tablespoon vanilla
3¾ teaspoons baking soda
3 cups low-fat buttermilk

Add and stir well:

2½ cups sifted flour (use whole
    wheat for all or part of the flour)
1½ cups flaxseed meal
1 cup cut-up dried apricots
1 cup or package of dried cranberries
1 cup dried cherries, optional
1 cup golden raisins
1 cup English walnuts or pecans, chopped
3½ cups Kellogg's Raisin Bran
1 cup chopped dates, optional

If the mixture looks thin, add more Raisin Bran. If it looks too thick, add a bit more buttermilk. Put in a large bowl with a tight-fitting lid. The mixture can be kept for about six weeks in the refrigerator. Bake them in a small muffin pan that is sprayed with nonstick spray or in a regular muffin pan with paper muffin cups. Cook at 350° to 375° about 15 to 20 minutes.

Charlotte Kaye Price-Hawkins

Born in Wichita, Kansas, Kaye has been living in Taylor County for fifty years. She graduated from Central High School in Columbia, Tennessee, with an interest in choir and drama club. As a child, Kaye wanted to be a performer. "I won the city and county 'Voices of America' speech contest during my junior year," shares Kaye. "My English teacher, in love with Shakespeare, had a bust of Shakespeare atop one of the cabinets. She would close her eyes and quote line after line. I remember being spellbound. I was in a beauty pageant when I was sixteen, and that was horrible, but a great step in the direction of learning how to be poised on the outside, even when I was shaking like a leaf on the inside."

She considers "a USO trip to the Far East while attending Pepperdine College, having two wonderful children who have grown up to be outstanding adults, surviving being a single parent for nineteen years, and then marrying a wonderful man after all those years and continuing to work, even in my seventies," some of the major events in her life. "After I retired from teaching, I began my own consulting business. I find great joy in helping teachers and students while having the freedom to give back to the community that I love."

"My daddy was a minister and my mother was the consummate preacher's wife— hospitable, gracious, and always smiling. Any visitor at church on Sunday would be welcome to come home with us, and special dinners were a staple in our home as I was growing up. One story mother likes to tell is that we were so accustomed to inviting people in for dinner that when a 'hobo' knocked on our back door one day while mother and daddy were gone, we girls invited him in to the kitchen and fixed him something to eat. When he finished eating, he said, 'Your momma and daddy are not going to be happy with you because you invited a stranger, and a man at that, into your home.' I said, 'Oh, no, they won't because we are entertaining an angel unaware.' He was right, though. My folks were *not* happy!"

"Our Sunday lunch was always roast with carrots and potatoes, green beans, rolls, and gravy. Nine times out of ten, we also had a Jell-O salad of some variety. During Christmas season during my high school years, we made English toffee because the kitchen had a marble counter, which was perfect for making that special candy."

About her community in the Big Country she says, "We are a community of caring people who love education, the arts, and philanthropy. Taylor County is an interesting place of diverse landscape and personalities. Wide-open lands are surrounded by highways and towns along the way.

"We love Perini Ranch Steakhouse for several reasons: the atmosphere and the food, of course. . . . But we love the 9/11 story about how Tom and his crew had cooked all night long on the tenth so that the big BBQ on the lawn of the White House would be ready for all of the special guests President Bush had invited. The morning of 9/11 changed America forever, but it didn't change the heart of Tom Perini. He and his crew had to evacuate the White House lawn quickly and decided that even though the event was cancelled, the food would still be enjoyed. So they took that marvelous food to one of the homeless shelters in DC and happily shared it with the men and women there. Another restaurant would be the Beehive, which serves great steaks as well. Oh, my! There are so many of my favorites—Copper Creek, Abi-Haus, Cypress Street Station, Hickory Street Café, and on and on.

"One of the best things about Abilene is the fact that we were named the Storybook Capital of Texas during 2015. Events at the Depot, the National Center for Children's Illustrated Literature, and the Grace Museum often rally the unique food trucks with their unique flavors and textures to cap off any street event. There will probably never be an event in Abilene that doesn't have some kind of food or beverage involved. But why not? Socializing around the table is the best time of all."

Jimmy's Thanksgiving Rolls

Dr. Jimmy Harelik, Comanche/Cross Plains

"I got this recipe from John and Alice Kay Arnet in Wyoming—friends of Patsy's and mine. John worked for the University of Wyoming as a pharmacist for the student health center and was on the faculty during the same time I was on the faculty. I taught fifth year pharmacotherapeutics and second year math." These are his family's favorite rolls.

1 cup milk

½ cup sugar

1¼ teaspoon salt

6 tablespoons shortening or butter, plus melted shortening for the dough

1 cup warm water

2 tablespoons sugar

2 packages yeast

3 eggs, beaten

6 cups flour

Scald milk; stir in ½ cup sugar, salt, and shortening. Cool to lukewarm; measure warm water and 2 tablespoons sugar into a bowl; sprinkle in yeast and let stand undissolved. Stir; add lukewarm milk mixture; add and stir in eggs. Add and stir in 3 cups flour, beating until smooth. Add and stir in 3 more cups of flour and knead.

Place in a greased bowl and brush the top lightly with melted shortening. Cover with a towel; let rise in a warm place until doubled in bulk, about 1 hour and 25 minutes; make out in any kind of rolls as you prefer (Dad dropped three round spoonsful in a sectioned muffin tin). Let rise maybe a half-hour and then bake 350° or 400° for 20 minutes.

Mexican Corn Bread

Connie Kirkham, Cross Plains

photo by Sassafras Company

Connie says she cuts back on the sugar to ¾ cup if serving with soup or stew.

- 1 cup melted butter (*not* margarine)
- 1 cup sugar
- 4 eggs
- 1 can chopped green chilies
- 1 large can cream-style corn
- 1 cup grated cheese
- 1 cup flour
- 1 cup yellow cornmeal
- 4 teaspoons baking powder
- 1 teaspoon salt

Combine and bake in a greased 9x13 pan for 20–25 minutes at 350°. Delicious!

photo by Sassafras Company

Navajo Fry Bread

Lola Molina, Buffalo Gap

Before Lola's was Lola's, it was Judy's. "Judy had sopaipillas on the menu," shared Lola. "But my mom made Navajo Fry Bread. So we changed the menu." The green enchiladas are her best seller, followed closely by her Navajo Fry Bread.

    2 cups white flour
    1½ cups whole wheat flour
    ½ cup sugar
    2–3 teaspoons baking powder
    mixture of equal parts water and milk
    vegetable oil for frying

Preheat oil in a frying pan. Mix all of the dry ingredients together. Add the water and milk mixture until you get a nice dough. Form the dough into balls and roll into small balls like you would for tortillas. Fry the bread in 350° oil until the bread has started to turn golden brown. Drain on paper towels and serve warm.

photo by Tiffany Harelik

Lola's in Buffalo Gap

Born in Zacatecas, Mexico, Lola came to Buffalo Gap in 1980 to look for her dad. "I liked it here, so I stayed," Lola told me while she was making breakfast tacos at her restaurant one morning. "I stayed here with my Uncle Javier. Judy Nalda had this place before me. I told her I would help her for two weeks washing dishes, and here I am still." She laughed about being at the restaurant nearly thirty years later.

"At that time, I was working for everyone in Buffalo Gap: babysitting for Nancy Perini, cleaning houses," Lola shared. She eventually took over the restaurant and changed the name from Judy's to Lola's in 1995.

"My name is Maria Delores, but my brothers called me Lola, so I kept it," she said about her name and the name of her restaurant. She married Oscar Molina, an Abilene High graduate.

Lola didn't miss a beat with our conversation as she rolled up a paper towel to light the gas grill. "You know I've been lucky since the day I left Mexico," she shared. "I told God, this is what I'm doing, and I'm leaving the rest up to you." Lola navigated her way through immigration and met someone who helped her get her papers. "He took me to Dallas, helped me get a doctor's appointment and everything. I went back to my hometown in Mexico to show off my papers," she said, smiling, while she opened a jar of fresh homemade salsa. Her faith continues to carry her through decisions, and the ups and downs of small-town restaurant ownership.

photo by Tiffany Harelik

Potato Refrigerator Rolls

Willie May Rider, Early

Like her handwritten recipe card reads, Willie May's Potato Refrigerator Rolls are "very good."

¾ cup shortening

¾ cup sugar

1 cup mashed potatoes

2 teaspoons salt

2 eggs

1½ cups warm water

2 packages dry yeast

5½–7½ cups flour

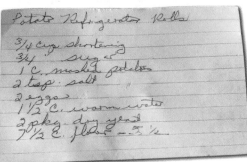

Cream shortening and sugar. Add potatoes and beat well. Add salt and eggs and beat more. Dissolve yeast in warm water and add it to the mixture.

Gradually stir in 5 cups flour. Knead in remaining flour. Cover and let rise until the dough has doubled in size. Punch down and place in a greased container.

Cover and place in refrigerator. Make into rolls 1½ to 2 hours before serving time. Bake on a greased pan after letting rise until doubled. Bake at 400° for a few minutes.

photo by Jeanette Floyd & Michelle Ring

Refrigerator Rolls

Mary Frances Morgan, De Leon, via Kay Harelik Morgan

"These were always present at a Morgan Thanksgiving or Christmas celebration. If not, there were lots of complaints." —Kay Harelik Morgan

Dissolve:

> 2 cups warm water
> 2 packages dry yeast

Then add:

> 2 eggs beaten (room temp)
> ¾ cup cooking oil
> ¾ cup sugar
> 1½ teaspoons salt
> 6 cups flour, unsifted and packed

Mix all together and stir enough to mix (not much). Leave the dough in the bowl, cover with a plate, and place in refrigerator for 4 hours before making out into rolls. Pinch off the amount of dough you want to use and roll it out on a floured board so the dough is about ½ inch thick. Cut circular rolls from the dough using the top of a cup and place in a greased, floured pan. Let rise 3 hours. Bake at 350° to 400° degrees. The unused dough will keep for about eight days in the refrigerator.

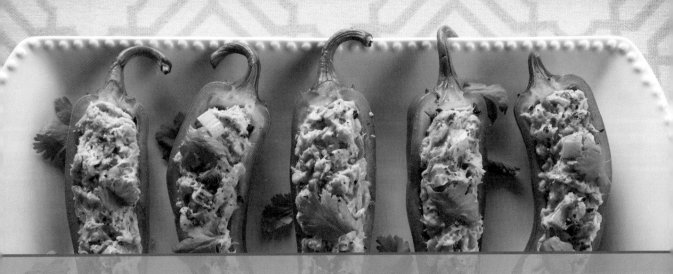

APPETIZERS
AND SNACKS

Baked Sandwiches
Jane Bonner, Cross Plains

Cheese Straws
Doris Jackson via Gavin Jackson, Abilene

Chorizo-Stuffed, Bacon-Wrapped Dates
Tiffany Harelik, Buffalo Gap/Cross Plains

Guacamole
Jane Bonner, Cross Plains

Olive Dip
Kaye Price-Hawkins, Abilene

Oysters
Jane Bonner, Cross Plains

Pecan Cheese Ball
The Texas Cowboys' Christmas Ball, Anson

Pimiento Cheese
Tiffany Harelik, Buffalo Gap/Cross Plains

Sausage Balls
Doris Jackson via Gavin Jackson, Abilene

Southwest Cheesecake Appetizer
Katie Browning, Abilene

Sweet and Sour Tapenade
Melanie Brown, Abilene

Thelma's Tuna-Stuffed Jalapeños
Sam Waring, Comanche

Baked Sandwiches

Jane Bonner, Cross Plains

These make a good addition to a buffet line while entertaining.

Preheat the oven to 350°. Take two packages fresh rolls and cut them in half horizontally. Place bottom halves of the rolls in a casserole dish.

On top of the bottom halves, place:

    1 pound shaved ham
    12 ounces cheddar and mozzarella

Heat in a saucepan:

    1 teaspoon Worcestershire sauce
    2 sticks margarine
    1–2 teaspoons dried onion flakes
    1 tablespoon poppy seeds
    3 tablespoons mustard
    1–2 teaspoons parsley flakes

Place top halves of rolls over the ham and cheese. Pour the liquid over the sandwiches. Bake 10 to 15 minutes at 350° until tops are golden brown.

Cheese Straws

Doris Jackson via Gavin Jackson, Abilene

photo by Sassafras Company

This recipe from Doris Jackson's Salad Buffet restaurant yields about 40 crackers.

    1 cup margarine
    1 cup grated sharp cheddar cheese
    ½ teaspoon salt
    1¼ cup flour

Preheat oven to 350°.

Cream the margarine, cheese, and salt together in a pastry blender. Add the flour slowly. Blend until smooth; form into rolls about 1 inch in diameter. Slice 1/8 inch thick. Place on an ungreased cookie sheet. Bake at 350° about 12 minutes.

photo by Sassafras Company

Chorizo-Stuffed, Bacon-Wrapped Dates

Tiffany Harelik, Buffalo Gap/Cross Plains

This is a fun and easy dish to bring to potluck Sunday night dinners. If you're not a fan of chorizo, you can trade out the chorizo for almond butter and sea salt. If you go the almond butter route, try popping a golden raisin or cranberry in the middle for a little extra flavor. I like to use nitrate-free, humanely raised or local bacon to get the healthiest bacon possible. Be careful to go through each pitted date and make sure their seeds are completely removed so you don't chip a tooth.

pitted dates
chorizo
bacon
toothpicks
maple syrup

Split the hollow dates down one side and pucker them open like little baked potatoes. Cook chorizo in a cast iron skillet for 10 to 15 minutes or until cooked through. While the chorizo is cooking, cut the raw bacon in thirds. Preheat the oven to 400°.

Let the chorizo cool enough to be able to work with it and then spoon dollops into the dates. Wrap the stuffed dates with raw bacon and insert a toothpick all the way through them. Line up the bacon-wrapped stuffed dates on a baking pan and bake at 400° for about 15 minutes or until bacon has cooked to a crisp. A few minutes before the dates are done, remove them from the oven and brush them with a little maple syrup. Then put them back in the oven to finish cooking.

I like the bacon extra crispy, but baking too long or having too much syrup tends to candy the dates, making them a little too chewy. It may take a few practice rounds before you get them the way you want them, but they are always a crowd-pleaser. Serve warm.

Guacamole

Jane Bonner, Cross Plains

Depending on the size of the avocados, this recipe can serve 4 to 6.

    2 avocados, pits removed
    salt, to taste
    juice of one lime
    1 medium tomato, diced
    3 tablespoons red onion, diced
    1 jalapeño, seeded and minced
    3 tablespoons fresh cilantro, chopped

Mash avocados and all ingredients in a bowl. Serve fresh with chips, carrots, cucumber slices, or whatever you like to use for dipping.

Olive Dip

Kaye Price-Hawkins, Abilene

"Serve with Fritos, Wheat Thins, Ritz Chips, or your favorite cracker." —Kaye Price-Hawkins

 1 large package of cream cheese, softened
 1 tablespoon (or to your liking) sour cream
 1 jar of whole green olives, drained
 1 large can of whole black olives, drained
 ¼ cup finely chopped onion, optional
 1 dash of your favorite seasoning (garlic salt, pepper, or whatever you want)

Chop up the green and black olives. I use a food processor; pulse them until they are chopped fine. If you let it run, you will have a paste! Then mix the olives and onion, if using, into the softened cream cheese and sour cream and seasoning.

Oysters

Jane Bonner, Cross Plains

This delightful Southern recipe offers a twist to the traditional Big Country table.

    salt, to taste
    pepper, to taste
    1–2 cups flour, as needed, depending on amount of oysters, plus 2 tablespoons
    oysters, as many as you would like
    2 tablespoons butter
    ¼ cup lemon juice
    2 tablespoons Worcestershire sauce
    ½ cup sherry
    1 cup A.1. Sauce
    3 tablespoons water

Mix salt, pepper, and flour. Dredge oysters in flour mixture and brown on both sides in a skillet over medium heat. Remove from heat.

In a bowl, mix butter, lemon juice, Worcestershire sauce, sherry, and A.1. Sauce. Pour sauce into a skillet on low heat (do not boil).

In a separate bowl, combine 2 tablespoons flour with 3 tablespoons water. Add to the sauce and stir. When sauce gets thick and warm, add the oysters. Serve warm.

Pecan Cheese Ball

The Texas Cowboys' Christmas Ball, Anson

This recipe by Rhonda Weaver is printed, with permission from the TCCB Association members, from *The Texas Cowboys' Christmas Ball Ranch Supper Cookbook*.

- 2 8-ounce packages of cream cheese
- 2 8.5-ounce cans of crushed pineapple, drained
- 2 cups pecans, chopped, divided
- ¼ cup green bell pepper, seeded and chopped
- 2 tablespoons onion, chopped
- 1 tablespoon seasoned salt

Soften cream cheese to room temperature. With an electric mixer, blend cream cheese, pineapple, 1 cup of pecans, bell pepper, onion, and seasoned salt. Chill well. Form into a ball and roll in pecans. Chill and serve with your favorite crackers.

Pimiento Cheese

Tiffany Harelik, Buffalo Gap/Cross Plains

"This is my mom's Aunt Marjorie's recipe. Marj's daughter Karen says the trick is to taste it often. We have used it to make sandwiches, spread it on crackers, and stuffed it in celery." —Tiffany Harelik

    1 pound Longhorn cheddar cheese, grated by hand
    ½ medium white onion, finely chopped
    1 small jar of pimiento
    enough mayonnaise to get the consistency spreadable (not Miracle Whip)
    salt, to taste
    pepper, to taste
    1 teaspoon or more jalapeño juice from a jar of pickled jalapeños

Sausage Balls

Doris Jackson via Gavin Jackson, Abilene

"What can be said about sausage balls?" reads this entry in Doris's recipe collection from the Salad Buffet. "They disappear faster than we can make them. We were just saying the other day, 'Do you suppose we can justify a Sausage Ball cook to the accountant?' Try them, you'll love them!" This recipe makes about 45.

    1 pound sausage
    1 10-ounce package cheddar cheese, grated
    3 cups Bisquick, dry

Preheat oven to 375°. Mix ingredients thoroughly. Shape into small balls (do not roll) and place in greased pans. Bake at 375° for 15 minutes or until brown.

Southwest Cheesecake Appetizer

Katie Browning, Abilene

photo by Catherine Thomas

The salty sweet softness of this dish makes it a great appetizer to serve with any Tex-Mex dinner.

Crust:

> 1½ cups crushed tortilla chips
> ¼ cup melted butter

Combine and press into a 9" springform pan. Bake at 350° for 10 minutes.

Filling:

> 16 ounces softened cream cheese
> 8 ounces shredded jalapeño jack cheese
> 3 eggs
> 1 cup sour cream, divided
> 4½-ounce can green chilies
> taco seasoning
> 1 cup picante sauce (see recipe in the Sauces and Jellies section)

Topping:

>   guacamole
>   pico de gallo

Combine cheeses in a mixer. Add eggs and ½ cup sour cream and mix well. Add taco seasoning, green chilies, and picante and mix to thoroughly combine. Pour mixture over crust. Place pan on baking sheet and bake 40 minutes. Cool 10 minutes and spread remaining sour cream in a thin layer on top of the cheesecake. Cool to room temperature and chill.

Use a small ice cream scoop to dollop the top with guacamole and pico de gallo. Remove the sides from the pan and transfer to a platter. Serve with chips.

Sweet and Sour Tapenade

Melanie Brown, Abilene

photo by Richard Fonvielle

This makes about 8 servings (about 1½ cups).

 1 10-ounce jar pitted kalamata olives (about 2 cups), drained
 ½ cup golden raisins
 2 tablespoons fresh basil, chopped
 1 garlic clove
 1 tablespoon drained capers
 1 tablespoon Dijon mustard
 ¼ cup olive oil
 fresh basil leaves to garnish
 pita chips

Coarsely chop olives, raisins, basil, garlic, capers, and mustard in a blender or food processor. Add oil gradually, continuing to pulse mixture until it is blended. Cover and refrigerate until ready to serve. Serve cold, with pita chips or other favorite food to dip.

Thelma's Tuna-Stuffed Jalapeños

Sam Waring, Comanche

The Dudleys were one of the local grandee families in Comanche. There were three brothers: Gail, Tom, and Eltos. (A local joke went that Tom ran the Chrysler dealership the brothers owned, Eltos ran the purebred Hereford cattle ranch, and Gail ran Tom and Eltos.) Tom and his wife Thelma were friends with my grandmother Frances Waring; they shared tourist trips to Mexico, had many common friends, and went to each other's parties.

One of Thelma's signature potluck dishes was pickled jalapeño peppers stuffed not with cream cheese or pimiento cheese, as was common, but with tuna. If Thelma came to a party, it was just about certain that she'd bring her tuna-stuffed peppers. Thelma and my grandmother are both many years gone, but today I'll sometimes make a batch of tuna-stuffed peppers and take it to a potluck, in memory of Thelma.

This recipe was adapted from the *Comanche Garden Club Cookbook*, 1967. The original recipe was made by Mrs. Tom Dudley.

24 jalapeños en escabeche,
    drained
6½ ounces tuna in water,
    drained
½ cup finely chopped pecans
mayonnaise, as needed

photo by Juliet Laney

Halve and devein the jalapeños. In a bowl, mix the tuna and pecans with enough mayonnaise to moisten. Stuff the jalapeño halves with a spoonful and arrange on a serving platter, not unlike deviled eggs. Adding diced pimientos or celery to the tuna is a nice touch as well.

SAUCES
AND JELLIES

Debbie's BBQ Baste
Debbie McInroe, Rising Star

Dried Fruit Compote
Brennan Vineyards, Comanche

George's Barbecue Sauce
George L. Minter Jr., Abilene, via Martha Minter Ferguson

Green Pepper Jelly
Jean McWilliams, Rising Star

Picante Sauce
Katie Browning, Abilene

Plum Jam
Ellen Webb via Carol Dromgoole, Albany/Abilene

Debbie's BBQ Baste

Debbie McInroe, Rising Star

Debbie used this recipe to compete with when she and her husband, David, participated in the Lone Star Barbecue Society cook-offs. They learned to cook the chicken "hot and fast" over charcoal using this baste.

1 cup honey
1 cup brown sugar
1 can peach or apricot nectar
several dashes Worcestershire sauce
1 stick real butter
1–2 cups KC Masterpiece Hickory Brown Sugar BBQ sauce

Mix everything together except the KC Masterpiece BBQ sauce. Add in a little of the BBQ sauce at a time until you reach the desired consistency. The sauce should run in a steady stream off the brush you are using to baste with. When ready to apply the baste, pat the baste on lightly with the brush. Do not "paint" the baste on—you don't want to wipe off any of the seasonings you have on the chicken.

Debbie and David McInroe

Debbie and her husband David moved to Rising Star from Stephenville in January of 2007. The first cook-off they placed in was with Debbie's goat at the Goldthwaite goat cook-off. Using her sweet and spicy rib rub, her goat took third and showmanship. "We won 125 dollars, but it might as well have been 1,000 dollars," laughed David when he told me the story. "We had been cooking for a year and a half before we placed." And at 50 dollars per entry, that can really add up with the cost of gas, meat, and preparation.

Debbie and David cook against each other in the same pit. Where David prefers Reo Spice company, Debbie uses Head Country's spices. "We decided we would go to one cook-off a month," David said. "Which was eight or nine cook-offs, since the organization takes the holidays off. But then we started going every other weekend and started doing better. So we went every weekend all over Central Texas."

The pair stopped cooking in 2005. "I had won a Grand Champion and I really wanted to end my cooking career with another," said David. "And I would have won it if my wife hadn't thrown my chicken in the trash," he said, laughing about the incident

photo by Tiffany Harelik

while Debbie in the next chair over grinned and said, "Oh, you're gonna tell that one again, are ya?" Debbie was the head judge at the event, and David wasn't going to let anyone accuse him of cheating. He found someone walking by to turn in his plates for him: seven ribs, seven slices of brisket, and a half chicken. That way none of the judges would know whose plate it was. "I didn't want to give it to one of our other competitors, because it would have been pretty easy to identify me if only one guy was turning in two entries," David shared. He needed to hit in all three categories to take home the Grand Champion, but one of the judges deemed his chicken was raw, albeit after it had passed through two other judges. David explained that the right thing to do to ensure everyone is comfortable after someone has claimed the entry is raw, is to toss it.

Although it would have been fun for David to take home the Grand Champion at that last cook-off, he had close to one hundred trophies from over the years. The accomplished cook shared that they ended up donating a lot of their trophies to a trophy company that could repurpose them.

One of the biggest tips they wanted to share for other home cooks and competition cooks is to thoroughly clean your pit between uses. "We pressure wash all the grease out and use a product called Greased Lightening. If you have your pit in the same shape every time, you'll have the same conditions to cook with each time. If you don't clean your pit and let the stalactites form, it makes the meat taste bitter.

"Don't hesitate to reach out and learn from the veteran cooks," they advised me. "That's how you learn."

Dried Fruit Compote

Sheila Wells of Brennan Vineyards, Comanche

photo by Rebecca Conley

½ cup dried apricots, chopped
½ cup prunes, chopped
½ cup dried cranberries
½ cup raisins
¼ teaspoon almond extract
zest of one lemon
Brennan's Lily Reserve or Viognier

Combine fruit, lemon zest, and almond extract. Dump it into a casserole dish. Cover it with the white wine. Don't be stingy—go ahead and cover it *good*! Like the fruit is swimming in it with lots more liquid than fruit.

Cover the dish with plastic and put in the fridge overnight. The fruit will rehydrate and soak up all the wine. Then just heat it up the next morning and serve it over waffles or French toast or English muffins or oatmeal. Of course, you can always just grab a spoon and eat it by itself!

Sheila Anne Wells

Currently living in Mills County, Sheila Anne Wells has been living in the Big Country all of her life. She graduated from San Saba High School in 1967 with thirty-eight in her class and played basketball, was on the drill team, was involved with stucco, belonged to the honor society, and was a class officer.

"I got the Betty Crocker Homemaker award when I was in high school and grew up in the 4-H organization," shared Sheila. "I love to cook; it is what I do. Cooking is my ministry; I love making people feel good through cooking.

"The ranch we live on has been awarded a Texas Heritage Award and has been in our family forever," said Sheila, who said she would like people to see that her community has rural roots that run deep. "In a small town we are a family," she said.

"I cooked for our family because my parents worked full-time jobs," shared Sheila. Fried venison and mashed potatoes and gravy were foods her family enjoyed on holidays and special occasions. "Lots and lots of salads and soups, too."

For food in her area, Sheila recommended the Priddy Gas Station for "the best hamburgers in the world." She also said that Star Beaus in Comanche is always good and has the "best" sandwiches.

George's Barbecue Sauce

George L. Minter Jr., Abilene, via Martha Minter Ferguson

"Sundays were spent watching our daddy baste chickens on the charcoal grill outside—almost a daylong process! They were always tender, juicy, and delicious!"
—Martha Minter Ferguson

1 pound salted butter, melted
1 14-ounce bottle ketchup
1 10-ounce bottle Worcestershire sauce
few drops Tabasco sauce
3 tablespoons lemon juice
2 teaspoons salt

Mix all together; cook 15 minutes to blend flavors. Makes enough to baste ten chickens or more when grilling.

Green Pepper Jelly

Jean McWilliams, Rising Star

Jean's mother, Rosealea, was the first president of the PTA in Cross Plains. A member of the Methodist church, she followed her mother as chairman of the Lord's Acre program. "This recipe is not hot unless you add more heat," shared Jean. "You can add red peppers to make a Christmas jelly. This will make 6 to 7 half-pints. We have sold this at the Lord's Acre for twenty years. It goes great over cream cheese, served with crackers, or over meat or red beans."

3–4 large green bell peppers, deseeded
1–2 fresh jalapeño peppers or more for more heat, deseeded
½ lime, juiced
a small amount of lime zest
a small amount of vinegar for blending the peppers
1½ cups white vinegar
6 cups sugar
1 bottle Certo (or other pectin)
green food coloring for darker green color (or red if you're doing a red pepper)

Blend peppers with some vinegar until well-blended. Bring lime juice, 1½ cups vinegar, and 6 cups sugar to a rolling boil that is bubbling up the sides of the pot. Add the pepper mixture in. Let stand five minutes. Add one bottle of Certo. Add your choice of coloring if desired.

Pour in jars to seal.

Picante Sauce

Katie Browning, Abilene

photo by Jeanette Floyd & Michelle Ring

"This is so fast and so delicious!" —Katie Browning

    1 14½-ounce can fire-roasted tomatoes
    3 Roma tomatoes, halved
    1 4-ounce can green chilies
    ¼–½ red onion, roughly chopped
    4–5 garlic cloves
    1 jalapeño, seeded
    juice of one lime
    ½ cup cilantro
    1 teaspoon salt
    1 teaspoon cumin
    ½ teaspoon cayenne

Combine all ingredients in a blender or food processor. Serve fresh with chips, or chill and serve cold.

Plum Jam

Ellen Webb via Carol Dromgoole, Albany/Abilene

"Ellen's plum jam is my favorite. It's tart, but not too sweet," shared Carol. "It's wonderful on toast or biscuits." This recipe is reprinted with permission from *You'll Be Going Back for Seconds* by Ellen Webb.

4 pounds plums
½ cup–1 cup water
1 box Sure-Jell (or other pectin)
8 cups sugar

Wash plums and remove any that are too ripe or cut off any bad places. Put in a large container and add ½ to 1 cup water. Simmer covered for 5 to 10 minutes. Pour cooked plums and juice in colander in large bowl. Mash to remove as much juice and pulp as possible.

Use 6 cups of juice (for softer jams add ½ cup more juice or water). Pour into a large pan and add 1 box Sure-Jell. Bring this to a hard boil and add 8 cups sugar, all at once, stirring until dissolved. Bring to a full rolling boil (a boil that cannot be stirred down). Boil hard for 1 minute, stirring constantly. Remove from heat. Skim off foam with a metal spoon. Pour into prepared jelly glasses. Clean edges of any spilled jelly. Melt and pour paraffin over top of each glass and seal. Will keep 6 to 12 months in a cool place. Makes 10 to 11 glasses.

SOUPS
AND STEWS

Battalion Beef Soup
The Texas Cowboys' Christmas Ball, Anson

Beef Stew
Connie Kirkham, Cross Plains

Chicken and Dumplings
The Texas Cowboys' Christmas Ball, Anson

Comanche Stew
Sam Waring, Comanche

Easy Potato Soup
Jessica Melson, Abilene

Lazy Eight Stew
Cathy Allen, Coleman

Potato Leek Soup
Mary Powell, Abilene

Battalion Beef Soup

The Texas Cowboys' Christmas Ball, Anson

Cook's note: A 15-gallon pot heated over a propane fish fryer for heat works well, as does a small canoe paddle for stirring. When the ingredients are purchased from a restaurant supply or membership warehouse like Sam's, it's an inexpensive way (60 to 70 dollars) to feed a small army (about 100, figuring servings at 16 ounces each). This makes a great fundraiser or appreciation meal. Taste during preparation, adding salt, pepper, and water.

This recipe by Clay Deatherage was printed with permission from the TCCB Association members from the *Texas Cowboys' Christmas Ball Ranch Supper Cookbook*.

25 pounds ground beef
½ pound salt
½ pound black pepper
1¾ pounds minced dehydrated onion
2 gallons tomato sauce
20 pounds frozen mixed vegetables
3 gallons water
1 pound beef flavor soup stock
4 gallons sliced new potatoes

Place ground beef, salt, pepper, and onions in a large pot and brown over high heat. Add tomato sauce and mix well. Add frozen vegetables, water, and beef stock and stir. Bring to a boil for fifteen minutes, stirring occasionally. Reduce heat and simmer approximately two and a half hours, stirringly regularly. Drain potatoes; add to soup, and then simmer an additional thirty minutes, stirring often.

Beef Stew

Connie Kirkham, Cross Plains

"Julio's Mexican Seasoning is a great winter season spice mix. Serve this stew with a pan of hot corn bread. Bless it and enjoy it!" —Connie Kirkham

- 1 pound ham
- ½ onion, diced
- 2 cloves garlic, chopped
- 1 cup beef broth
- 1 cup water
- 2 stalks celery, diced
- 2 large potatoes, diced
- 2 carrots, cut in rounds
- 1 bag frozen or fresh corn
- 1 bag frozen or fresh green beans
- 1 bag frozen or fresh English peas
- ½ head of cabbage, shredded
- 1 can diced tomatoes in liquid
- 1 small can tomato sauce
- salt, to taste
- pepper, to taste

Sauté ham with onion and garlic until onions are translucent and meat is cooked through. Drain fat. Add all remaining ingredients and simmer on medium-low heat for at least thirty minutes or up to several hours.

Chicken and Dumplings

The Texas Cowboys' Christmas Ball, Anson

"We have a ranch dinner prior to Michael Martin Murphey's concert each year. With a ticket you get to have dinner with Michael and his Rio Grande Band plus go to his dance. We feed around 130 each time, and the Association members do all of the cooking. This is a favorite of Michael Martin Murphey and the Rio Grande Band when they perform at the Cowboys' Christmas Ball in Anson, Texas." —Rhonda Weaver.

This recipe was printed with permission from the TCCB Association members from the *Texas Cowboys' Christmas Ball Ranch Supper Cookbook*.

6–8 cans of cheap biscuits (store-bought)
1 whole chicken, washed and the inside packaging removed
salt and pepper to taste

In a large stew pot, add the washed, whole chicken (breast side down) with enough water to cover the bird. Bring the water to a boil. Turn the heat to medium high and continue to cook the chicken for 15 to 20 minutes. Carefully turn the bird over with the breast meat up. Continue to cook until the leg quarters start falling off. Remove the chicken and let it rest on a platter to cool.

While the chicken is cooling, add enough water to bring the broth level to 2 to 3 inches below the rim. Turn the heat on high until boiling again. Open your cans of biscuits and tear each one into four pieces. Carefully add them into the boiling chicken broth. Stir after each can of torn biscuits is added. Be sure to stir, scraping the bottom of the pot so they will not stick. Once they are all added to the broth and appear to be done, turn the heat down low.

Debone the chicken and chop the chicken meat into small bite-sized pieces. Add to the dumplings and stir. Salt and pepper to taste. The sauce will be thin at this point. Turn the heat off and let them sit covered. When the dumplings cool, they will thicken.

Eat with corn bread, crackers, and pickles.

A West Texas Original

The Texas Cowboys' Christmas Ball

photo by Rhonda Weaver

Submitted courtesy of Rhonda Weaver; reprinted with permission from the TCCB Association members.

In 1885, M. G. Rhodes hosted a wedding party and dance at his Star Hotel in Anson. Larry Chittenden, a salesman and writer, was visiting his uncle in Jones County and attended. He was so inspired by the dance held that night for the cowboys and ladies that he composed a poem commemorating the occasion: "The Cowboys' Christmas Ball."

In 1934, Leonora Barrett and Hybernia Grace revived the historic ball and its folklore.

This 131-year-old winter holiday celebration includes traditional western music, poetry, dancing, listening, refreshments, and fellowship. Historic Pioneer Hall (and museum) at Anson has been the Ball home since completion of its construction in 1940. The Ball and Hall are designated an official state historical event and site by the Texas Historical Commission to promote its historic preservation and celebrate its Texas history.

The Ball was memorialized by rancher and poet Larry Chittenden with his famous poem "The Cowboys' Christmas Ball." The poem with music was later published in the John Lomax classic *Cowboy Songs & Other Frontier Ballads*. The song was first performed at the 1946 Ball by cowboy folklorist Gordon Graham. The Ball is portrayed in the large 1930s mural at the Anson Post Office and in the 1930 watercolor painting by Maxine Walker Perini on permanent display at Abilene's Grace Museum. Pulitzer Prize-winning novelist Edna Ferber recognized the "Cowboys' Christmas Ball at Anson in Jones County" in her memorable novel *Giant*. There is also a permanent historical exhibit of the Ball and Hall in the Southwest Collections Library at Texas Tech University in Lubbock.

The preeminent history of the Ball and its origin, preservation, and continuation has recently been written by Dr. Paul H. Carson, professor of history at Texas Tech University. It is a classic, impeccably researched, historically accurate, and thoroughly documented story titled *Dancin' in Anson: A History of the Texas Cowboys' Christmas Ball*.

The Ball is also the acknowledged genesis for the Cowboy Christmas concerts throughout the country performed by America's number one cowboy singer Michael Martin Murphey and his Rio Grande Band. They have highlighted the Ball one night each year for the past twenty-one years. Muddy Creek is the faithful house band that has played the other two nights for many years.

I have to stop for a second and tell you specifically about one family that has come every year for twenty-one years just for Michael Martin Murphey. The first year that Michael came, this family with a four-year-old, a two-year-old, and a week-old baby drove from the Dallas area. The mother is a Home Economics teacher and fashioned matching outfits for her, the girls, and even Dad. This tradition has continued through this last Christmas. They now reside just south of San Antonio. The family got out of school, jumped in the car, and drove as hard as they could on Thursday of the Ball. They arrived just in time for Grand March at 9 P.M., then danced and visited until midnight. The girls put on their traveling clothes, brushed their teeth, and climbed back in the car with their pillows and blankets for the drive home to arrive in time for school to take their finals.

This is my fortieth year as a board member. In those years, we have worked very hard to make the three nights fun and family-friendly. Santa even stops by for a visit and dance or two on Saturday night and always has a saddlebag full of candy for everyone. Nothing is sweeter than seeing little boys or girls dancing with their parents. This is what the Ball is about. Making memories!

1885 Ball rules remain in effect. Ladies are required to wear dresses on the dance floor. Gentlemen must check in hats, spurs, and guns. And yes, in recent years we *have* had guns checked at the door! No drinking, smoking, spitting, fighting, cussing, or riding horses is allowed in the Hall.

photo by Rhonda Weaver

Comanche Stew

Sam Waring, Comanche

"In the 1960s, our family's insurance agency (Waring Insurance in Comanche) would throw an annual potluck dinner party in October at Windy Hill Farm for our customers and our friends (often the same people)," shares Sam Waring. "My father, Joe Waring, would spend the afternoon out in the back lot overseeing two washpots full of Comanche stew, simmering to feed all the guests." After fifty years, he still remembers the verse from one year's invitation:

> "Soup's on!" the cook was heard to cry;
> An autumn chill was in the sky.
> It's time to eat Comanche stew.
> (Perhaps we'll eat some crackers, too.)
> So dress up warm, come eat your fill,
> We're cooking stew at Windy Hill.

This recipe was adapted from the Comanche Study Club Cookbook, 1927. The original recipe was by Mrs. F. E. Adams.

    5 pounds beef stew meat
    3 pounds bacon or salt pork
    4 pounds stewing chicken
    3 pounds rabbit, dressed weight (optional)
    game birds: dove, quail, or whatever you have (optional)
    1 pound squirrel, dressed weight (optional)
    12½ cups tomatoes
    7½ cups whole kernel corn
    7½ cups green peas
    4 large onions
    3 chilies anchos, seeded for less heat
    8 pounds potatoes
    2 pints oysters
    salt and pepper to taste
    cayenne to taste

Put all meat and the chilies in a stew kettle (for the parties, we used an old cast iron washpot over an open fire) in water to cover, and cook for 2 to 2½ hours. Remove and bone the meat and set aside, discarding the bones. Sieve the stock and discard any remaining bones.

Add the potatoes, tomatoes, and onions and cook for about half an hour before adding the corn and peas. The oysters should be added about 15 minutes before the stew is removed from the fire, and may be left out entirely. The stew should cook in all about four hours.

photo by Tiffany Harelik

Sam Waring

Sam Waring was born in Brownwood (which had the nearest hospital in 1957) and was raised in Comanche, Texas. "I'm a collateral descendant of the Captain James Cunningham family; the Cunninghams were among the first settlers in Comanche County," Sam shared. "My maternal great-great-grandfather Robert H. Tate and Cunningham matriarch Susannah (Susie) were brother and sister.

"My father's family owned 220 acres four miles south of Comanche, on a hill overlooking Lake Eanes, which my grandfather John D. Waring Jr. was the project engineer for. It was known as Windy Hill Farm (not the same as the organic farm/ranch of the same name today).

"My great-grandmother Tavia McArthur was an excellent Southern cook, which served her when she had to take in schoolteacher boarders to feed herself and raise her daughters (Nima Tate and Ava Gore). My own parents and our housekeeper made sure I learned some things about practical cooking, rightly believing that because I was likely to live as a bachelor for a while, I needed to learn how to take care of myself on a daily basis. This meant lessons not only in cooking but in cleaning, laundry, and simple clothing repair. (I used all of those lessons.)

"My immediate family didn't have any great cooks, but my father's fascination with the Orient and Eastern food (he served in the Pacific during World War II and in Japan during the Occupation) raised my general curiosity."

Sam was in band four years, was a member of National Honor Society, and acted in a one-act play district competition. There were eighty-one students in his graduating class from Comanche High School in 1975. After high school, Sam left Comanche for Austin where he attended the University of Texas.

As a kid growing up in Comanche, Sam said he wanted to be a librarian, following the example of his mother, who was director of the Comanche Public Library for fifty-six years (1960–2016). He's now a technical analyst at Dell Inc., "in an irremediably obscure back-office position," Sam said. "I consider this a success."

Easy Potato Soup

Jessica Melson, Abilene

photo by Catherine Thomas

"This is my mother-in-law's recipe that we would make every week if we could. My family of five all loves it. We have tweaked it to our taste." —Jessica Melson

1 package O'Brien hash brown potatoes
4 cups water
3 bouillon chicken cubes
1 can cream of chicken soup
½ pound Velveeta cheese, cut into pieces
optional add-ins: 1 can of chicken, corn, or green chilies

Cook potatoes in 4 cups of water and the bouillon cubes until tender about 10 to 20 minutes. Add soup and Velveeta cheese along with any add-ins. We always add chicken.

Serve when cheese is completely melted.

Lazy Eight Stew

Cathy Allen, Coleman

"The Allen family has been operating the Lazy Eight Ranches for several generations both in Coleman County and in South Texas," shared Cathy Allen. "Currently, the Lazy Eight operates in several Texas counties utilizing large pastureland along the Colorado River and Jim Ned Creek Valley to irrigated and dry land wheat ground. The Lazy Eight is headquartered out of Coleman, Texas. Abbi Allen is the sixth generation to work on the ranch and enjoy the ranching life in Coleman County."

Cook's note: The beef we use for Lazy Eight Stew is grass-fed Lazy Eight beef. I usually add about 2 tablespoons of flour or other thickener to my wine and stir before adding it to the stew if I want a little more body.

2 pounds beef sirloin, cut in 1-inch cubes
¼ cup cooking oil
3 large carrots
3 potatoes, cubed
1 10-ounce jar tomatoes in glass
4 cups beef broth
2 tablespoons dried oregano
1 onion, diced
1 tablespoon minced fresh garlic
1 teaspoon salt
1 teaspoon pepper
2 4-ounce cans green chilis
1 cup red wine
1 tablespoon cumin

photo by Cathy Allen

In a large skillet or Dutch oven, heat oil over medium heat. Brown the meat and remove from pot. In that same pot, cook the onions and garlic for about 5 minutes or until softened. Return meat to the pot along with the rest of ingredients. Season to taste. Bring to a boil and reduce heat to a simmer. Simmer partially covered for 2½ hours or until meat is tender.

Potato Leek Soup

Mary Powell, Abilene

"I first tasted potato leek soup at a bed and breakfast just outside Fredricksburg, Texas. It tasted so good that I came home and tried to re-create it. After looking through recipes and making it several times, I came up with this recipe that we have enjoyed many times, especially on cool evenings." —Mary Powell

3 leeks, washed well and chopped

3 garlic cloves, chopped

3 stalks celery, chopped

2 jalapeños, chopped, optional

4 tablespoons butter

1 tablespoon olive oil

Sauté ingredients in oil and butter until tender.

Add:

3–5 carrots, diced

3 russet potatoes, peeled and diced

4–5 Yukon Gold potatoes, peeled and diced

2 cans chicken broth

salt and pepper to taste (add plenty of pepper)

Cook until potatoes are tender.

Add:

2 cups milk or half and half

Cook on low heat for 10 to 15 minutes, stirring to keep from sticking. Use an immersion blender to reach desired consistency. Top with grated cheese and serve.

photo by Tiffany Harelik

SIDES

Acorn Squash Mash
Olivia Clardy Tyler, Abilene

Beth Morgan's Seven-Layer Salad
Beth Morgan, De Leon, via Kay Harelik Morgan

Broccoli Rice Casserole
Willie May Rider, Early

Corn Casserole
Kaye Price-Hawkins, Abilene

Cranberry Salsa
Loretta Newberry, Potosi, via Emily Gilmore

Jessica's Favorite Green Chile Hominy
Perini Ranch Steakhouse, Buffalo Gap

Maggie's Salad
Maggie Meers, Hamby

Maw Maw Harelik's Cottage Cheese
Side Dish
Kay Harelik Morgan, Comanche

Paw's Squash Dressing
Elizabeth Hiller via Emily Gilmore, Abilene

Potluck Grape Salad
Tiffany Harelik, Buffalo Gap/Cross Plains

Rafter 3 Beans
Mary Miller via Susan Allen, Coleman

Roasted Brussels Sprouts
Carla Garrett, Abilene

Roasted Sweet Potatoes
Roxie Thomas, Cross Plains

Rustic Corn Pudding
The Texas Cowboys' Christmas Ball, Anson

Squash Casserole
Paulette Foster, Cross Plains

Sweet Potato Casserole
Margaret Henderson, Coleman

Veggie Pack
Mike and Janna Hardwick, Rising Star

Acorn Squash Mash

Olivia Clardy Tyler, Abilene

"This recipe offers an alternative to loaded mashed potatoes." —Olivia Clardy Tyler

2 larger acorn squash
bacon, cooked crispy (amount is up to you)
chives or green onion, chopped (amount depends on just how much you care for onion)
grated cheese of choice
heavy cream
real butter

Cut each acorn squash in half, and deseed using a regular table spoon. Put a pat of butter inside each squash and put halves back together. Microwave on high for roughly 6 to 7 minutes. Turn each squash over using a large kitchen towel (they will be very steamy and can be hot). After turning the squash halves over, microwave them again for about 6 to 7 minutes (the time can vary quit a bit, depending on the size of the squash and microwave). Once soft, like a cooked potato, use your large kitchen towel again to hold the steamy squash and scoop out the insides into a large saucepan.

photo by Tiffany Harelik

Mash up the squash to the texture of mashed potatoes. Add butter if squash seems dry. Add heavy cream until your preferred thickness is reached (more cream for a runnier consistency, less for thicker). Turn the heat to medium under the saucepan. Add chopped chives or green onion, crispy bacon pieces, and grated cheese. Stir fairly often. Your mash is ready to be served as soon as the cheese is melted, and all is mixed in evenly. Wah-lah! An alternative to loaded mashed potatoes!

Olivia Clardy Tyler

Born and raised in Abilene, Olivia Clardy Tyler graduated from Wylie High School and went to college at Texas Tech in Lubbock, eventually landing in Comal County close to the Guadalupe River. "I am a stay-at-home mom now, but for six years before my first child, I was a teacher/coach," shared Olivia. During her Wylie years, she played basketball, ran track, and sang in the choir and show choir. She gave a nod to the Liv and Daron Prank Holly Squad. About her contribution, she shared: "I just like to cook. I rarely measure. I enjoy creating my own stuff, and I really like doing that all on my own."

Beth Morgan's Seven-Layer Salad

Beth Morgan, De Leon, via Kay Harelik Morgan

photo by Mary Lancaster

"This salad was always present at a Morgan Thanksgiving or Christmas celebration. If not, there were lots of complaints." —Kay Harelik Morgan

Place the following in a large glass bowl (it looks pretty in a trifle dish) in the order given.

> leaf lettuce, torn in pieces
> fresh spinach, torn in pieces
> 5 green onions, chopped
> 1 box frozen green peas, thawed
> 5 slices of bacon, fried crispy and crumbled
> 3 hard-boiled eggs, chopped

Dressing:

> 8 ounces sour cream
> ½ cup mayonnaise
> small package Good Seasons Italian dressing mix

Cover and refrigerate, preferably overnight.

Broccoli Rice Casserole

Willie May Rider, Early

This is Willie May's version of a Big Country classic side dish.

    1 10-ounce package chopped broccoli
    ½ onion, finely chopped
    ½ green pepper, deseeded and finely chopped
    ⅛ cup melted margarine
    ½ jar Cheez Whiz
    1 can cream of chicken soup
    ½ cup cooked rice (plain)
    ½ teaspoon garlic salt

Preheat the oven to 350°. Thaw broccoli. Sauté the onion and pepper in the margarine on low heat for approximately 10 minutes. Add Cheez Whiz and soup. Simmer 10 more minutes. Add garlic salt and mix well.

Pour in cooked rice. Pour the mixture into a baking dish and cover it with foil. Bake, covered, at 350° for 20 minutes.

Corn Casserole

Kaye Price-Hawkins, Abilene

"This dish is the one requested dish at every family meal we have at our house. My grands *love* it! If you want ideas for the rest of the dinner, try ham, a salad of your choice (we love fresh baby spinach salad with poppy seed dressing, sliced strawberries, slivered honey roasted almonds, and craisins) and green beans or broccoli. Yummy!" —Kaye Price-Hawkins

This casserole yields approximately 8 to 10 servings. Preheat oven to 350° while you mix well these ingredients in the order they are listed in a large bowl:

    2 cans creamed corn
    2 eggs
    1 package of corn bread mix (I like the packaged white corn bread mix)
    ½ cup chicken broth
    3 tablespoons sour cream
    2 tablespoons melted butter
    ½–1 cup of shredded cheese (half cheddar and half shredded Parmesan)
    1 package of frozen white corn
    salt, to taste
    pepper, to taste
    small dash of garlic salt (optional)

Pour the mixture into a greased 9x13 glass baking dish and bake for approximately 45 minutes depending on your oven. I cover the mixture for about 20 minutes and then finish cooking uncovered. You will know when it is done, as the top and sides will be a little bit brown. To check the middle, use a toothpick to see if it is done. You don't want it to dry out, but you don't want it to be mushy.

Cranberry Salsa

Loretta Newberry, Potosi, via Emily Gilmore

photo by Sassafras Company

"Christmas must-have! Mom's cranberry salsa. It's good with smoked or fried turkey, or on tortilla chips. Mom adds more jalapeños and onions to hers." —Emily Gilmore

1 12-ounce package fresh cranberries, finely chopped

1 9-ounce can crushed pineapple, drained

⅔ cup sugar

½ cup green peppers, finely chopped and seeded

2 tablespoons onions, finely chopped

1 jalapeño pepper, seeded and chopped

¼ teaspoon salt

Jessica's Favorite Green Chile Hominy

Perini Ranch Steakhouse, Buffalo Gap

Reprinted from *Texas Cowboy Cooking* by Tom Perini with permission from Tom and Lisa Perini.

"A Perini Ranch Steakhouse signature dish, this recipe was developed with the late Mrs. Louise Matthews of Albany, Texas, to go with the brisket at her annual party. We visited, considered a whole list of ingredients, and after a little trial and error, Green Chili Hominy was born. It really looks good on a plate; in fact, for large parties we sometimes serve it in cast iron for a more rustic effect. And it's versatile: it's great for breakfast or brunch, a light lunch, or as a side dish with almost any entrée. And it can be prepared ahead of time, frozen, and reheated, and it is just as good."

1 cup chopped onion, sautéed
4 15-ounce cans white hominy
　　(drain and reserve liquid)
½ cup hominy liquid
1 tablespoon juice from pickled
　　jalapeños
½ pound cheddar cheese, grated
10 slices bacon, fried crisp and
　　chopped (reserve drippings)
1 cup chopped green chilies
1–2 pickled jalapeños, seeded and
　　chopped (optional)

photo by Tiffany Harelik

Sauté the onions in a little of the bacon drippings and put aside. Heat the hominy in a separate sauté pan with half of the cheese and the jalapeño juice, stirring often. When the cheese melts, add half the peppers (chilies and jalapeños) and bacon, all the onion, and hominy liquid. Pour into a 9x13 baking pan and sprinkle with the remaining cheese, bacon, and peppers. (At this point, it can be refrigerated or even frozen, if you want to make it in advance.) Bake at 325° until the cheese on top melts, about 15 minutes (or 40 minutes, if refrigerated). Serves 10 to 12.

Maggie's Salad

Maggie Meers, Hamby

This is a family favorite from Maggie's family. She suggests storing about half of the dressing in the refrigerator for another use, as this makes quite a bit.

Dressing:

1 cup sugar
1 cup oil
3 tablespoons soy sauce
½ cup red wine vinegar

Mix all ingredients together until the sugar is dissolved. Store in the refrigerator.

Salad:

romaine lettuce
pecans, chopped and sautéed a few minutes until crispy
ramen noodles, sautéed a few minutes until crispy

Toss salad ingredients together with about half of the dressing. Serve cold.

Maw Maw Harelik's
Cottage Cheese Side Dish

Kay Harelik Morgan, Comanche

Kay writes me, "The recipe you're looking for is actually one *my* grandmother made—my maw maw (Daddy's mom). It's real easy. You take a large container of cottage cheese and mix in an 8-ounce block of cream cheese and an egg. Bake in a 350° oven until it browns a little bit on top. You can dollop a bit of butter on top before you bake it if you want. That's about it."

large container cottage cheese
1 8-ounce block of cream cheese
1 egg
dollop of butter, optional

Preheat oven to 350°. Mix cottage cheese and cream cheese together with an egg and pour in a baking dish. Add a dollop of butter on top if desired. Bake 15 to 20 minutes or until the top starts to brown.

Paw's Squash Dressing

Elizabeth Hiller via Emily Gilmore, Abilene

This is Emily's grandmother's recipe. She is known as "Paw."

2 cups cooked squash
½ stick margarine, melted
1 large onion, chopped
1 can cream of chicken soup (undiluted)
2 cups crumbled corn bread
salt, to taste
pepper, to taste
poultry seasoning, to taste

Preheat oven to 400°. Drain and mash cooked squash. Combine all ingredients in a casserole dish and bake 30 to 40 minutes at 400°.

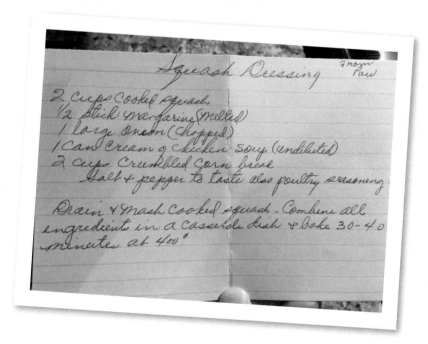

Potluck Grape Salad

Tiffany Harelik, Buffalo Gap/Cross Plains

"This is one of my favorite dishes to bring to a large potluck, or to give as a neighborly or celebratory gift. I tend to pour extra balsamic in mine because I like it tart. You can add crumbled feta if you like." —Tiffany Harelik

1 package red seedless grapes
1–2 cups chopped pecans
1–2 tablespoons balsamic vinegar
1 teaspoon honey

Whisk honey and balsamic together and set aside. Cut half of the red grapes in half and leave the rest whole. Toss the grapes and pecans in the dressing. Serve chilled.

Rafter 3 Beans

Mary Miller via Susan Allen, Coleman

"The Rafter 3 is an historic Coleman County Ranch established by J. P. Morris in 1884. The descendants of J. P. Morris are still operating the Ranch today." —Cathy Allen

For 2 cups of beans:

2 cups beans
salt, to taste
pepper, to taste
1 clove garlic, chopped
2 strips of bacon

photo by Cathy Allen

Pick and clean beans very carefully. Sometimes they have rocks or mud clods—discard them along with any shriveled up beans or any beans that are discolored. Rinse beans in cold water.

Put rinsed beans in a large pot with at least 8 cups water. Be sure beans are covered with at least 2½ to 3 inches of water. Add salt, pepper, garlic, and bacon. Bring to a boil and lower heat and continue to slow boil. Stir occasionally. Add water at least once while cooking. Cook 2 to 2½ hours before adding sauce. Beans should be cooked down and have little juice before adding sauce.

Sauce:

½ medium onion, diced
bacon grease or butter
1 can whole tomatoes
3–4 tablespoons Brer Rabbit Syrup (full flavor)
3–4 tablespoons apple cider vinegar
soup spoon full of chili powder (Gebhardt's)

Sauté onion in bacon grease or butter. Add tomatoes and break them up with your spoon while stirring. Add remaining ingredients except beans. Cook down on low heat until you have a thick consistency. Stir occasionally. Add to beans and simmer together for 30 minutes.

Roasted Brussels Sprouts

Carla Garrett, Abilene

photo by Juliet Laney

any amount of fresh brussels sprouts
olive oil
garlic, minced
sea salt

Preheat oven to 400°. Put cleaned brussels sprouts on cookie sheet. Drizzle olive oil and sprinkle minced garlic (amount up to you) and sea salt on top.

Optional additions include bacon bits, pepper, and (after removing from oven) sprinkled, shredded Parmesan cheese.

Bake in oven for 40 minutes at 400°.

Roasted Sweet Potatoes

Roxie Thomas, Cross Plains

"I'm always looking to add healthier recipes to my menu. This has quickly become a frequently requested dish from my family." —Roxie Thomas

    4 sweet potatoes, cubed
    ⅓ cup olive oil
    ¼ cup honey
    2 teaspoons cinnamon
    sea salt, to taste
    black pepper, to taste

Preheat oven to 375°. Place sweet potatoes in large bowl. Add olive oil, honey, cinnamon, salt, and pepper. Mix together with your hands to get potatoes covered.

Spread evenly on baking sheet. Roast for 25 to 30 minutes until brown and tender. You may wish to sprinkle with extra olive oil before serving.

Rustic Corn Pudding

The Texas Cowboys' Christmas Ball, Anson

If you're preparing this dish in advance, cool it completely, then cover and refrigerate. Reheat in microwave just until warmed through. This recipe by Cindy Spraberry was printed with permission from the TCCB Association members from *The Texas Cowboys' Christmas Ball Ranch Supper Cookbook.*

1 14 ⅓-ounce can cream-style corn
1 16-ounce bag frozen corn
1 16-ounce container sour cream
⅓ cup cornmeal
3 large eggs, separated
½ teaspoon salt
⅓ teaspoon pepper

Preheat oven to 350°. Grease a 9x13 glass or ceramic baking dish, or a 4-quart oval dish; set aside.

In a large bowl, combine cream-style corn, frozen corn, sour cream, cornmeal, egg yolks, salt, and pepper. In a small bowl, with mixer on high speed, beat egg whites until stiff peaks form. Fold egg whites into the corn mixture; pour into prepared baking dish. Bake pudding 45 minutes, or until edges are set and center jiggles slightly. Let stand on a wire rack 10 minutes to set before serving.

Squash Casserole

Paulette Foster, Cross Plains

This recipe makes approximately 8 servings.

1 package cornmeal

3 yellow squash, cooked, drained, and cut into bite-sized pieces

1 onion, chopped

½ cup green bell pepper, chopped, optional

2 tablespoons butter

1½ cups grated cheddar or Monterey jack

3 eggs, beaten

1 teaspoon salt

1 small jar pimiento pepper, optional

½ teaspoon pepper (black or white)

Preheat oven to 350°. Mix all the ingredients together. Bake at 350° for 25 minutes.

Sweet Potato Casserole

Margaret Henderson, Coleman

photo by Jeanette Floyd & Michelle Ring

This sweet potato casserole warms up any hearty dinner.

Beat:

> 6 tablespoons butter, softened
> ½ cup sugar

Add:

> 2 beaten eggs
> 1 teaspoon vanilla
> ½ cup milk

Mix in 3 cups mashed sweet potatoes (from 4 medium potatoes).

Topping:

> 1 cup brown sugar, packed down
> ⅓ cup flour

Mix together the brown sugar and flour. Cut in 2 tablespoons softened butter until like caramel. Pour over potatoes. Cover topping with 1 cup chopped pecans and pat down. Bake at 350° for 45 minutes.

Veggie Pack

Mike and Janna Hardwick, Rising Star

This versatile recipe is a great addition to any backyard BBQ.

8–10 slices bacon

Opus sausage (precooked), sliced in
 ¼-inch rounds

5 large red potatoes, skin on and sliced
 in rounds

2 sweet onions, sliced in rounds

2–3 jalapeños, deseeded and diced finely

2 yellow squash, sliced in rounds

1 zucchini, sliced in rounds

1 pound corn (frozen or fresh)

1–1½ pounds okra (frozen or fresh)

1 bell pepper (green or red), sliced

½ head green cabbage, sliced

2 sticks margarine

2 tablespoons Montreal steak seasoning, or to taste

1 tablespoon Morton's Season-All seasoned salt, or to taste

1 tablespoon garlic salt, or to taste

photo by Kevin Dunn

Fry the bacon several minutes until it's about three-quarters of the way cooked. Pour the grease from the bacon into a 12x18 aluminum pan with the drippings and partially cooked bacon pieces. Add all other ingredients and toss to distribute spices and coat evenly.

Cover tightly with aluminum foil to keep everything moist while it's cooking. Put the covered dish on the grill on medium heat. Stir occasionally and cook about 45 minutes to an hour, or 2 to 3 beers, according to how fast you drink.

MAIN COURSES

Alaskan Salmon Salad
Paulette Foster, Cross Plains

Alice Roby's Dove
Connie Kirkham, Cross Plains

Barbecued Brisket
The Texas Cowboys' Christmas Ball, Anson

Brent's Brisket in the Oven
Brent Bush via Hailie Harelik Hubbard, Early

Chicken and Wild Rice
Mary Powell, Abilene

David's Perfect Texas Brisket
David McInroe, Rising Star

Ellen Webb's Fried Chicken
Ellen Webb via Carol Dromgoole,
Albany/Abilene

Family-Style Sausage
and Peppers
Jerrod Medulla, Abilene

Italian Stewed Pork Chops
Tiffany Prier Lamb and Judy Voelter, Abilene

Lasagna to Die For
Angie Wiley, Abilene

Mamie's Party Hamburgers
Mary Pittman Minter, Abilene,
via Martha Minter Ferguson

Mom's Spaghetti
Katie Browning, Abilene

Parmesan Chicken
Ellen Webb via Carol Dromgoole,
Albany/Abilene

Patty's Enchilada Stack
Patty Rogers, Hawley

Poppy Seed Chicken
Julia Porter Bramblett, Abilene

Quail on the Grill
Connie Kirkham, Cross Plains

Rosealea's Chicken Salad
Jean McWilliams, Cross Plains

Scrambled Hamburger Salad
Doris Jackson via Gavin Jackson, Abilene

Shredded Beef Tacos
Maggie Meers, Hamby

Slow Cooker Enchiladas
Jami Anders, Rule/Abilene,
via Stephanie Anders Hood, Abilene

The Beehive's Chicken
Fried Chicken
Nariman Esfaniary and Aaron Perez, Abilene

Turkey, Dressing, and Gravy
Ellen Webb via Carol Dromgoole,
Albany/Abilene

Venison Bourguignon
Brennan Vineyards, Comanche

Venison over Noodles
Connie Kirkham, Cross Plains

Venison Piccata
Erin Maloney Schroeder, Abilene

Wagyu Chicken Fried Steak
Jean McWilliams, Cross Plains

Alaskan Salmon Salad

Paulette Foster, Cross Plains

photo by Juliet Laney

The Foster family has been in the Cross Plains area for more than one hundred years. This recipe comes from Paulette, who learned to make this when her husband James was working in Alaska.

> flaked salmon (one can or fresh-caught, cooked)
> ¼ cup onion, diced
> ¼ cup celery, diced
> 2 tablespoons sweet pickle relish
> 1 heaping tablespoon mayonnaise
> 1 teaspoon black pepper

Optional, add ½ cup each:

> green or red grapes
> walnuts or pecans
> apples

Mix all ingredients. Serve on crackers or toast.

Paulette and James Foster

One of Paulette's friends told her, "James wants to meet with you. Just go to lunch with him; you don't have to marry him." Accordingly, the couple went to a park to have a picnic for their first date. "He brought his mother Louise's fresh homegrown tomatoes, and I knew I was in love," Paulette shared.

Paulette and James lived in Prudhoe Bay, Alaska, from 1983 to 1994. James continued to commute between Texas and Alaska until 2003. "The trip took eleven hours, and he did it every two weeks," Paulette shared. "Being from Odessa, I never thought I would live in the country," Paulette said, "but I love it. Louise introduced me to everyone and the people are great." She shared that Louise was an active member in the First Baptist Church. "She was a quilter, wonderful cook known for her pies and cakes. She entertained the preacher every Sunday," said Paulette.

James's great-grandfather W. W. (Wiley Wood) held a special place in Texas history. He was one of 19 children, born on December 31, 1844, when Texas was a republic and Anson Jones was the President of the Republic of Texas. After fighting in the Texas Revolution as part of the original 300 Sam Houston led down to fight against Mexico, W. W. was captured and released, eventually returning to Jasper County where he married Claressa Crockett, the widow of Davey Crockett's brother. She was fifteen years older than W. W. They relocated to Callahan County where James's grandfather Steve settled the property the family lives on now. Their property comprises 1,000 acres and has been in their family for more than 100 years.

James told a story about the Comanche and Kiowa that were living close to the Foster family homestead. "They had come to steal the horses and cattle, so our family was keeping them in stalls. Grandpa hid behind the tree when the Indians came to ambush and kept reloading his rifle to fend off the Indians. In the morning, they found ten arrows stuck in the tree he was hiding behind."

The Foster family history runs deep in Texas. Another family member, Randolph Foster, was hired by William B. Travis and Sam Houston to hunt game and provide the soldiers with meat during the Texas Revolution (1835–1836). Additionally, John Foster (James's great-great-great grandfather) had the distinguished honor of working for George Washington as his chaplain on the Potomac.

Alice Roby's Dove

Connie Kirkham, Cross Plains

"These are tender, delicious, and very moist. You can cook quail the same way."
—Connie Kirkham

Place birds on a cookie sheet. Dry with paper towels, then season with salt, pepper, and garlic salt to your taste. Roll lightly in flour. In a skillet, brown the birds in a little olive oil. Place the birds in a greased casserole dish with a lid. Bake at 300° for 15 to 20 minutes, depending on the size of the birds.

Barbecued Brisket

The Texas Cowboys' Christmas Ball, Anson

This recipe by Rhonda Weaver was printed with permission from the TCCB Association members from the *Texas Cowboys' Christmas Ball Ranch Supper Cookbook*.

- 1 6–8 pound beef brisket
- ½ of 3-ounce bottle of liquid smoke
- 1 teaspoon celery salt
- 1 teaspoon onion salt
- 1 teaspoon garlic salt
- 1 cup water
- ½ cup brown sugar
- 1 cup ketchup
- 2 tablespoons flour

Marinate brisket in liquid smoke, celery salt, onion salt, garlic salt, and water overnight. Bake, covered, in preheated 250° oven for 5 hours. Cool meat. Blend drippings, brown sugar, ketchup, and flour in a saucepan. Bring dripping mixture to a boil, stirring constantly. Slice brisket and cover with sauce. Bake at 300° for one hour in preheated oven.

Brent's Brisket in the Oven

Brent Bush via Hailie Harelik Hubbard, Early

"This is the recipe I typed up from my father-in-law. He never does anything the same, so it is completely adjustable and forgivable. Where it calls for orange juice, 7Up, or ginger ale . . . it is an option of any one of those. He uses whatever is on hand. Feel free to alter or adjust where needed." —Hailie Harelik Hubbard

Start with 3 to 4 pounds of brisket, with the fat cut off. Adjust the following measurements as preferred. Use the juices as a gravy and serve warm.

Marinade:

> 2–3 tablespoons Worcestershire sauce
> 2–3 tablespoons soy sauce
> a little A.1. Sauce, if you have it
> 1 cup orange juice, 7Up, or ginger ale
> 2 teaspoons garlic salt
> 2 teaspoons onion salt

Heat up all the marinade ingredients in the microwave 15 to 20 seconds to help dissolve and mix the spices well. Place the meat in a glass pan and let soak in the marinade, covered with foil, in the refrigerator overnight.

Preheat the oven to 200° or 350° depending on how quickly you want to cook the brisket. Sprinkle the meat with garlic salt and onion salt. Place the covered pan in the oven. To cook the meat faster, bake at 350° for the first hour and then turn down the temperature to 250° until done, a few more hours. To cook overnight, bake on 200° all night.

Chicken and Wild Rice

Mary Powell, Abilene

"This recipe was shared with me about forty years ago by my sweet sister-in-law and great cook, Sylvia McCaleb. It is a tried and true recipe that I have used through the years and have shared many times. It is great served with hot bread and a fruit salad!" —Mary Powell

    2 cups diced chicken
    1 package Uncle Ben's long grain and wild rice (prepared according to directions)
    1 can French style green beans, drained
    1 can cream of celery soup
    1 can water chestnuts, drained
    1 small jar diced pimiento
    1 cup grated mozzarella cheese

Combine all ingredients. Heat at 350° until bubbly, about 30 minutes. Top with cheese and heat until melted, 5 to 10 minutes.

Mary McCaleb Powell

Born in Abilene, Mary McCaleb Powell has lived in the Big Country her entire life. "I have lived in Anson, Ballinger, and Abilene, but always in the Big Country," she said. "I played basketball, volleyball, and tennis and ran track during high school at Anson. I was in the Spanish club, Future Homemakers, and Future Teachers of America." There were about sixty-five students in her graduating class in 1969, of which she was the valedictorian. Some of her favorite memories from growing up in the Big Country include: "We once made forty-six points in a high school basketball game. I helped my brother butcher and freeze fifty chickens for his FFA project. I lived in the very hometown of the famous Anson Ghost Lights. I once milked our Jersey cow Jezebel with the help of my older brother, who later was the mayor of Abilene during the 90s.

"I moved away from Anson for college, but came back married with children in the 80s for the oil field surge. My father and husband did abstracting and sur-veying in Jones County," said Mary. "I always wanted to be a wife and mom, but I also thought it very important to have a college degree and a career path if needed. So teaching became my career choice. I am teaching kindergarten, which I love to do! I am retiring after about thirty years of teaching—twenty-six in kindergarten and four of teaching home economics in high school."

She considers marrying Bishop Powell one of her greatest life events, as well as "having three great kids (who have perfect spouses) and eight wonderful grandkids! My husband is a great musician, and our children inherited his musical gifts. They play together in a family band and travel the countryside."

"My husband's family was among the first settlers in Coleman, Concho, and Runnels Counties," she said. "We moved and rebuilt their 136-year-old rock house at the confluence of the Concho and Colorado Rivers, to keep it from being cov-ered by the waters of Lake O. H. Ivie in 1990. We visit the house very often, and my husband would like for us to reside there in retirement.

"The cooks in both my husband's and my family really appreciate recipes that have lasted several generations, and very few weeks go by that we do not have some dish that has been a mainstay in the family. On holidays, especially, every dish is from a recipe that we've heard our parents and grandparents talk about having when they were small. All our meals were from scratch. My mom and Bishop's mom did not bake out of a box, and they always tried to use fresh ingredients. When we lived in Ballinger and Anson, we fed out our own calves. In our family, I became the bread baker. I bake yeast rolls on holidays, and I have made sourdough bread, cinnamon rolls, and whole wheat bread from starter for thirty years."

About her community in Abilene, she said, "It is a very friendly place to live, and (besides having constant water rationing) is a pleasant place to live. It is a wonderful place to raise children and is filled with wonderful people!"

David's Perfect Texas Brisket

David McInroe, Rising Star

David McInroe is a celebrated and decorated cook among the Lone Star Barbecue Society in Texas. This is his award-winning recipe for brisket.

Cut about one pound of fat off the brisket, keeping about 3/8 of the fat on the flat part. Start the pit at 400°. Season the meat with desired seasonings. David and Debbie used to cook against each other in competition. He preferred Reo Spices and she used Head Country spices.

Sear the seasoned meat fat side down for 30 minutes, then sear it meat side down for 30 minutes. Reduce the heat to 325° and let the brisket lay in the pit for about an hour to relax it.

Put the brisket in a large foil pan. Pour one can of apricot nectar in the bottom of the pan, and place the meat side down in the nectar. You need the liquid in the bottom of the pan so the meat doesn't burn. Place foil over the pan and seal to make a little oven. Do not wrap the brisket tightly in foil; leave plenty of air, but do seal the container completely.

Allow the internal temperature of the brisket to increase 10 to 12 degrees per hour. Monitor this with a digital probe thermometer. When the brisket's internal temperature hits 190° to 195°, the temperature will come to a standstill and hold steady if you do nothing else. So at this point, kick the temperature up to 350° to 400° until you see the internal temperature start to rise again. Once it starts to rise, lower the temperature down to 300°. Even though you have lowered the temperature, it will still cook. Once you reach 203° to 205°, your brisket is done.

Slice it with the grain and serve warm.

Ellen Webb's Fried Chicken

Ellen Webb via Carol Dromgoole, Albany/Abilene

"Her fried chicken is *excellent*! She's holding a platter of fried chicken on the cover of her cookbook. Funny story—she had fried up a batch of chicken so we could take the picture. Went to the photo studio (Terry Hughes used to have a studio in downtown Abilene) . . . and he took pictures. Then he said, 'Ellen, I've just got to ask you—can I have a piece of that chicken?' Terry purchased cookbooks that year to give to all of his important clients.

"When we published her cookbook, we only printed two hundred. We were primarily planning to just give it to friends and family . . . no big deal. However, when the book came out, the newspaper did a little feature story

photo by Hughes Photography

about it, and we were down to forty copies in no time! And that was prior to a big book signing we had planned at our store (Texas Star Trading Company) the following Saturday (this was in December 2007, right before Christmas). We ended up limiting people to purchasing one copy, and then we gave them color cards that they could use to give to people to tell them that a copy of the book would be coming! We couldn't get more printed until January. That was very stressful! She then had a book signing in Albany (where my parents lived forever and where I grew up) early that next year (January or February, I can't remember) . . . and sold several hundred copies of the cookbook." —Carol Dromgoole

This recipe is reprinted with permission from *You'll Be Going Back for Seconds* by Ellen Webb.

"I learned to fry chicken when my mom had to go to work during the depression. My dad taught me how to kill, clean, and cut up a chicken." —Ellen Webb

"Move over Colonel Sanders 'cause Aunt Ellen's Texas Fried Chicken and her country gravy are the best!" —Nancy Webb, niece

"Ellen's fried chicken is the greatest—and it passes the ultimate test: it is as good cold as it is hot." —Glen Dromgoole, son-in-law

Use either a whole chicken cut up in desired pieces or a chicken cut up by the grocery store. (I prefer cutting up the whole chicken, using one that weighs 3¼–3½ pounds). After washing it several times, I put it in a bowl and salt it generously, letting it stand overnight or several hours in the refrigerator before cooking. Rinse well, add salt and pepper, and dredge in flour.

I use a large cast iron skillet with plenty of Crisco and bacon drippings (2 to 3 tablespoons). Have grease very hot, adding pieces of chicken until pan is full but not crowded. As soon as the chicken begins to cook, turn heat down to medium and cover. Check after 3 to 4 minutes to be sure it isn't getting too brown. Turn when golden and continue to fry until all pieces are golden brown. If you are cooking livers and gizzards, be sure to use a fork and punch holes in them to prevent popping.

For the cream gravy, pour most of the grease into a heatproof container, but leave brown crumbs in the pan. Add 3 to 4 tablespoons of flour and brown; add salt and pepper and then whisk in enough milk to make a nice consistency.

Family-Style Sausage and Peppers

Jerrod Medulla, Abilene

Jerrod graduated from Wylie High School and now has a professional career in the music industry. He plays Americana, Texas Roots, blues guitar, and southern twang. This is one of his family recipes.

6 hot Italian (fennel) sausage links
6 sweet Italian (fennel) sausage links
1 medium red bell pepper, cut in long ½-inch strips
2 large yellow bell peppers, cut in long ½-inch strips
1 large yellow onion, cut in half and then in long ½-inch strips
1 small clove garlic, crushed
3 thin slices prosciutto, chopped
3 to 4 large yellow potatoes, skinned and cut into bite-size pieces
1¼ teaspoon oregano
¼ teaspoon white pepper
¼ cup olive oil
1 tablespoon butter
1 tablespoons white wine (medium flavor)
black pepper, to taste
salt, to taste
freshly grated pecorino cheese

Preheat oven to 375°. Start heating a large cast iron skillet. Add just enough water to cover the bottom of the skillet. Add sausage links to the pan to simmer—make sure you turn the sausage to heat evenly and then poke holes in the sausage and cook in the fat to brown until cooked.

In a separate nonstick pan, add your olive oil and heat the pan. Add the crushed garlic to the oil for 1 minute, or until garlic is light brown. Remove the garlic and finely dice. Add the butter and chopped prosciutto to the oil. Lightly brown the prosciutto and then add the onions. Cook onions for about 3 minutes on medium-high heat. Add the wine, turn heat to medium, and then cook for another 3 minutes or until the wine is evaporated. Add the bell peppers and cook on medium-low for about 12 to 15 minutes.

Throw in your potatoes, oregano, salt, pepper, and diced garlic. Let the potatoes sauté on low to medium-low for about 10 to 15 minutes while turning every few minutes. Should get a nice crust. (Do not let burn.) Once sausage is cooked, remove and cut links in half. Add the sausage to the rest of the ingredients and mix into a casserole dish. Cover with foil and cook for 20 to 30 minutes or until the potatoes are tender. Top with freshly grated pecorino cheese.

Italian Stewed Pork Chops

Tiffany Prier Lamb and Judy Voelter, Abilene

photo by Kevin Dunn

"This is my mom Judy Voelter's recipe." —Tiffany Prier Lamb

1 garlic clove
½ teaspoon salt
½ teaspoon pepper
2 tablespoons olive oil
1–2 carrots, sliced
2–3 celery stalks, chopped
1 cup dry red wine
2 beef bouillon cubes
1 14-ounce can whole peeled tomatoes OR stewed tomatoes
6 boneless trimmed pork chops

Brown garlic and pork chops in oil. Add carrots, salt and pepper, and wine. Simmer covered over low heat for 30 minutes or until carrots are tender.

In another pot, cook celery in bouillon until tender; drain. Add celery and tomatoes to pork mixture for last 10 minutes of cooking time. Serve warm.

Tiffany Prier Lamb

Born in Independence, Missouri, Tiffany Prier Lamb moved to Taylor County in 1977. "I moved to Abilene when my father was transferred here with Phillips Petroleum," Tiffany shared. "I always loved living in the Big Country. I was never one of those kids who wanted to leave and never return as soon as I was old enough. I did, however, leave to attend college in Waco at Baylor University in 1988 and graduated in 1992. I was hired at Continental Airlines in 1995 as a flight attendant. I always wanted to travel while keeping Abilene as my home base.

"I lived in Newark, New Jersey, and Cleveland, Ohio, and also was in Houston for a time, but I always missed Abilene and the Big Country. People are great everywhere, but no one is as friendly as people in Texas, and specifically the Big Country! People here trust God and fellow man. They keep their word, and are always willing to help their neighbor. Taylor County is beautiful in a special way. Mesquite trees, red dirt, and rolling plains. I love the terrain!

"My mom is a wonderful cook," Tiffany shared, "but she doesn't really like cooking. I actually really enjoy cooking, and I think spending time with my grandparents in Missouri and watching both of my grandmothers in the kitchen inspired me. I like cooking a lot when there is time to create.

photo by Whitney Jeleniewski

"I grew up eating wholesome foods like pot roast, brisket, pork chops, chicken, homemade spaghetti sauce, etc. At Christmas we always made homemade sugar cookies and had fun decorating them. That was always the best!"

I asked Tiffany to share more about the restaurants in the area. She said, "We always take guests to Perini Ranch Steakhouse in Buffalo Gap. They have the best steak in the universe! Truly! Growing up, we went to Crystal's Pizza and Spaghetti. I defy you to find someone who grew up in Abilene in the 70s and 80s who didn't know about Crystal's! They had awesome pizza and themed rooms. The entrance was a cave! So fun!"

Lasagna to Die For

Angie Wiley, Abilene

"This was one of my first recipes to learn as a young married woman. This is a great recipe to eat one and freeze one. It's easy to prepare ahead and clean up all before dinner." —Angie Wiley

Boil 6 lasagna noodles. Have one 16-ounce package shredded mozzarella ready for layering. In a separate skillet, brown and drain:

1 pound lean ground meat

Add:

1 tablespoon dried parsley
1 teaspoon basil
½ teaspoon salt
¼ teaspoon pepper

Add:

1 16-ounce can Italian seasoned diced tomatoes
1 8-ounce can tomato sauce

Let simmer uncovered 20 to 30 minutes.

Meanwhile, combine in small bowl:

1 cup cottage cheese
1 egg
2 teaspoons parsley
2 tablespoons grated Parmesan cheese
½ teaspoon salt
½ teaspoon pepper

Begin layering in this order in an 8x8 casserole dish:

½ of the cooked noodles
½ of the cottage cheese mixture
½ of the mozzarella
½ of the meat mixture

Repeat. Bake at 350° for 30 minutes.

Angie Wiley

Angie Wiley came to Abilene in 1982 to go to Hardin-Simmons University, where she met her husband, Rob. "We left in 1987 after undergrad and came back in 1995 and have been here ever since!" said Angie.

"One of my most life-changing events was meeting my husband. We had such a fun and exciting two years dating and engagement. Now thirty years and three children later, we are still going strong. My upbringing in the love of family and my Heavenly Father gives me the foundation to live and love.

"I taught school for five years. Right before our second child was born, we made the decision for me to stay home with the kids. I have been a stay-at-home mom for twenty-two years, and we just now became empty nesters. I stay busy volunteering in the community and serving in my church and Abilene schools.

"Growing up, my family was centered around simple meals that my working parents could always have on hand and prepare after working long days and weeks. I am always looking for easy to prepare and simple meals that can be made ahead and that have quick prep and easy cleanup. I have a collection of favorites we leaned on during our hectic years when the kids were young. I like menus with ingredients that I can always have on hand.

"Mom cooked a great chicken fried steak, and my dad grilled delicious steaks. We seemed to have mostly meat and potatoes because my dad didn't like casseroles. My grandmother always baked a red velvet cake for Easter in the shape of a bunny, and I could always count on that cake again on my birthday.

"The top request for special occasions in our family is definitely Perini Ranch Steakhouse. We also love the Beehive, Abi-Haus, Cypress Street Station, and Bogie's. Abilene is a strong community that is full of good, solid people. We have a zoo, museums, and wonderful art, and we are the Storybook Capital of Texas!"

Mamie's Party Hamburgers

Mary Pittman Minter, Abilene, via Martha Minter Ferguson

photo by Tiffany Harelik

"It was always a special occasion when Mamie (Mary Minter) fixed party hamburgers for us!" —Martha Minter Ferguson. This recipe yields about three burgers.

    1 pound ground beef
    ¾ cup buttermilk
    1 large egg
    1 small onion, chopped
    ¾ teaspoon salt
    ⅛ teaspoon dried thyme
    ⅛ teaspoon pepper
    dash garlic salt
    1 tablespoon prepared mustard
    6 slices gouda cheese
    3 whole wheat hamburger buns, halved

Combine all ingredients except the hamburger buns and gouda cheese, mixing thoroughly. Let mixture stand about 30 minutes to blend flavors. Spread the uncooked mixture on the 6 hamburger bun halves, spreading out to the edges.

Place on unoiled baking sheet or broiler pan, meat side up. Broil about 15 minutes, or until meat is cooked to desired stage. During last 2 minutes of broiling, place two slices of gouda cheese on top of the meat. Serve hot.

Mom's Spaghetti

Katie Browning, Abilene

"This was a childhood favorite of mine and now my boys love it!" said Katie. Her mom, Ibby Jones of Waco, Texas, used to make it for her. "My brother and sister remember my mom drying pasta all over the house. I'm the third child and she started getting store-bought with me!" —Katie Browning

1½ pounds ground beef

1 small onion, chopped

3 garlic cloves, pressed or chopped

8 ounces tomato sauce

6 ounces tomato paste

2 cups tomato juice

¼ cup red wine or water

1 tablespoon chili powder

2 teaspoons salt

1 teaspoon sugar

1 teaspoon pepper

1 teaspoon ground oregano

photo by Katie Browning

Brown beef with onion over medium-low to medium heat (you can add chopped bell pepper and/or 8 ounces sliced mushrooms here with the onion if you'd like). Cook until liquid has evaporated, or drain if there's too much liquid. Add garlic and cook a few minutes. Add remaining ingredients and stir well. Bring to a boil. Cover, reduce heat, and simmer 30 minutes.

Serve over your favorite pasta (or spiraled zucchini "noodles" if you're feeling fancy).

Parmesan Chicken

Ellen Webb via Carol Dromgoole, Albany/Abilene

photo by Tiffany Harelik

Ellen says, "My grandchildren always want this when they come to eat at my house." This recipe is reprinted with permission from *You'll Be Going Back for Seconds* by Ellen Webb.

Prepare crumb mixture:

    4 slices white or whole wheat bread (make crumbs in blender)
    ¾ cup Parmesan cheese, can add more
    ½ teaspoon garlic salt, can add more
    1 tablespoon parsley flakes, can add more

Wash and drain the amount of chicken needed to serve guests. Use all of a whole chicken cut into pieces, or several of one cut, like breasts, thighs, legs, or a combination. Lightly salt.

Melt 1 stick margarine. Dip chicken pieces into melted margarine, then roll in bread crumb mixture. Place in ovenproof dish. Drizzle a tiny bit of water around edges of dish. Cover and bake 1½ hours at 275°. Remove cover and bake 10 to 15 minutes longer at 350°.

Patty's Enchilada Stack

Patty Rogers, Hawley

photo by Tiffany Harelik

"I'm from Abilene, and I have taught at Hawley High School since January 2013. I also taught at Clack Middle School from 1992 to 2003. This is a favorite recipe with my family, and my students in culinary arts at Hawley High School make and sell them as a fundraiser. They have always been very popular." —Patty Rogers

2 pounds ground beef

1 small onion, chopped (I haven't been adding onions to mine that I sell)

1 10½-ounce can cream of chicken soup (or substitute)

4 ounces green chilies, chopped

1 package or ¼ cup taco seasoning

12 (or more) corn *or* flour tortillas

Brown beef and onion. Drain grease and return to skillet. Add soup, green chilies, taco seasoning, and ¾ cup water. Simmer for 15 minutes or more. In a small casserole dish, began layering ingredients in this order: meat mixture, grated cheese, and torn-up tortillas. Repeat. I like to end with meat mixture on top. Typically, you will have 3 layers of meat and 2 layers of tortillas.

Cheese sauce:

    1 cup (approximate) shredded cheddar cheese

    8 ounces Velveeta

    ½ stick butter

    3 tablespoons flour

    2 cups milk

    4 ounces green chilies, chopped

In a large saucepan, melt butter, add flour, and stir till blended and thickened. Gradually add milk and stir continuously. This will make a gravy. Once gravy is complete, add cheese and green chilies and continue to stir and heat until to desired thickness. This will burn on the bottom, so be careful by stirring continuously.

Pour cheese mixture over enchilada stack and sprinkle with grated cheese. Cover and freeze.

Alternately, you can bake immediately at 350° for about 30 minutes until bubbly (if casserole has been in refrigerator overnight, then cook for about 1 hour). I like to cover with foil and check on it. Cook from frozen for two hours.

Poppy Seed Chicken

Julia Porter Bramblett, Abilene

"I grew up with my mom making this, and it has always been a favorite. It's one of those recipes that has been passed down and is just notes written on a scratch piece of paper—which I think are the best recipes!" —Julia Porter Bramblett

4 whole cooked chicken breasts, shredded,
    or 1 whole cooked chicken, deboned (what I prefer)
1 tablespoon poppy seeds
white sauce
2 sleeves Ritz crackers
butter

White sauce:

2 tablespoons butter
2 tablespoons flour
salt, to taste
pepper, to taste
1 cup milk or 1 cup chicken broth
1 cup sour cream
    (room temperature is best)

photo by Mary Lancaster

For the white sauce, melt the butter. Add flour and stir constantly until bubbly. Whisk in the milk or broth until smooth and thick consistency. Salt and pepper to taste. Remove from heat and whisk in the sour cream until smooth.

For the topping, crush 2 sleeves of Ritz crackers in a gallon Ziploc bag. Melt 3 tablespoons of butter in a pan (may need more or less). Add the crackers, coat the crackers with butter, and cook until a golden brown.

Preheat oven to 350°. Add the cooked chicken and poppy seeds to the white sauce and mix together. Spread into a baking dish. Shake the topping over the chicken. Cook for 30 to 40 minutes until bubbly.

Quail on the Grill

Connie Kirkham, Cross Plains

Coat the bird with olive oil and season with a good steak rub. Cook on an open medium-heat grill until done. Don't overcook. When done, place in foil-sealed container until ready to serve.

If time allows, marinate birds overnight in plain yogurt with ½ cup Italian dressing. Pat dry and follow above directions. This ensures moist meat.

This overnight marinade also works great with chicken. It's best with plain yogurt and Italian dressing, but you can add herbs and spices like basil, rosemary, thyme, oregano, and so on to your taste to the yogurt. The chicken breast will nearly double in thickness and will be very moist and tender.

Rosealea's Chicken Salad

Jean McWilliams, Cross Plains

"This family recipe from my mother won a 4-H contest." —Jean McWilliams

2½ cups cooked chicken, diced
1 cup celery, diced
1 cup white grapes, sliced
2 tablespoons parsley, minced
1 teaspoon salt
1 cup mayonnaise (or less, to taste)
½ cup cream, whipped

Fold the whipped cream into the mayonnaise and toss all ingredients with the mixture.

Scrambled Hamburger Salad

Doris Jackson via Gavin Jackson, Abilene

This recipe from Doris Jackson's recipe collection from her Salad Buffet restaurant in Abilene is one of her grandchildren's favorites. "This is so versatile," her recipe reads. "Serve hot or cold as a side dish, or spread on bread for a sandwich. Serves 8."

1 pound hamburger, browned, drained, and crumbled
1 dill pickle, diced
1 onion, diced medium
¼ cup mayonnaise
2 tablespoons prepared mustard
salt, to taste
pepper, to taste

Toss all ingredients together.

The Salad Buffet:
Doris Jackson

Doris's grandson Gavin Jackson shared her recipe collection, which included this excerpt that sheds light on her former restaurant, the Salad Buffet.

The Salad Buffet was opened in October of 1974 as a culmination of a long-time dream. After thirty-eight years of nursing, I decided it was time for a new and different life. Always the thought had been for a tearoom, but one morning out of the blue came the idea of serving salads only.

The forty-eight-year-old house that was our home was the perfect setting to create an atmosphere of gracious dining. This is the goal that we try to maintain—excellent food served in beautiful surroundings, with quiet music and subdued conversation. Our patrons remark continually that they come because of the peaceful atmosphere as well as the excellent food.

The table is laden with a variety of salads, served in beautiful antique and Depression glass dishes. Some of the patrons spend as much time admiring our serving dishes as they do eating the food.

These comments would not be complete without my saying thank you to all of you that have told or written me your favorite recipes. You will find many of them included here. We hope that you will enjoy the recipes as much as we have.

Sincerely,
Doris Jackson

Shredded Beef Tacos

Maggie Meers, Hamby

Try Maggie's shredded beef tacos for your next Taco night. She suggests serving on warm tortillas or making this nacho style on chips.

1 beef shoulder roast

1 can green chilies

½ cup (more if desired) salsa

2 tablespoons cumin

1½ tablespoons chili powder

1 teaspoon paprika

1 teaspoon garlic powder

1 beef bouillon cube

salt, to taste

pepper, to taste

tortillas for serving

salad slaw, to taste per serving

juice of ½ lime, fresh squeezed over each serving

shredded cheese, to taste per serving

sour cream, to taste per serving

Season meat with dry seasonings. Place in slow cooker with beef bouillon cube, green chilies, and salsa. Cook on low for 5 to 6 hours. When meat is done and tender, take it out to cool and shred it up when you are able to handle the meat. You can add more juice from the slow cooker if the meat is too dry.

We serve on warm tortillas or make nacho style. Top the meat with slaw, fresh lime juice, shredded cheese, and sour cream.

Slow Cooker Enchiladas

Jami Anders, Rule/Abilene, via Stephanie Anders Hood, Abilene

Stephanie sent in her mom Jami's recipe for slow cooker enchiladas. These are great to prepare in the morning and let them cook all day for family dinner.

1 pound lean ground beef
1 cup onion, chopped
½ cup green bell pepper, chopped
1 can kidney beans, drained
1 can black beans, rinsed and drained
1 teaspoon chili powder
½ teaspoon ground cumin
½ teaspoon salt
¼ teaspoon pepper
1 can Rotel, undrained
⅓ cup water
2 cups Monterey jack cheese, grated
1 dozen flour tortillas
Sour cream, lettuce, tomatoes, and olives for condiments

In a skillet on medium heat, cook beef, onions, and green pepper until beef is browned and vegetables are tender, approximately 5 to 10 minutes. Drain. Add the rest of the ingredients except the cheese, tortillas, and condiments.

In a slow cooker, layer tortillas (usually two is enough to cover the bottom), beef mixture, and cheese. Repeat until all ingredients are used. Cover and cook on low 6 to 7 hours.

Serve with sour cream, lettuce, tomatoes, and olives or other condiments you desire.

The Beehive's Chicken Fried Chicken

Nariman Esfaniary and Aaron Perez, Abilene

photo by Tiffany Harelik

Widely recognized for their chicken fried steak, the Beehive's Abilene location also cooks up chicken fried chicken on Tuesdays. They serve it with a country-style gravy that contains flour, milk, chicken broth, cream, salt, pepper, and garlic. This recipe serves 12.

12 8-ounce boneless, skinless chicken breasts, tenderized
vegetable oil for frying

Breading mixture:

3 parts flour
1 part Italian bread crumbs
Beehive house seasoning

Egg wash:

½ gallon milk
4 eggs

Heat oil to 350°. Dip the chicken breast into the flour mixture, into the egg wash, and then into the flour mixture again. When the oil is hot enough, place the coated chicken in the oil to fry until golden brown.

The Beehive

Ali Esfandiary came to the United States from Iran in 1966, followed by his brother Nariman in 1972. Over the years, they had worked in the restaurant industry, which, along with soccer scholarships, got them through school. In 1982, they were driving through Albany, Texas, and saw the restaurant that had been closed for two years.

"The bank wouldn't give us a loan," Nariman shared with me at the Beehive Abilene location one morning. "We offered to pay the restaurant owner's (Bill Smalley) bills and see if we could get it going again. If not, no big deal." And Mr. Smalley agreed. "Then we asked him to co-sign a loan to help us pay for the first month of groceries to get going. He said half-jokingly, 'Now you've asked too much. I don't even know if you boys can cook,' which was true. So we invited him to dinner.

"We were driving back from Albany and I looked at my brother. I said, 'How much money do you have?'

'Ten dollars,' he said. 'What about you?'

'Five dollars. Well, what are we going to cook him with 15 dollars?'"

They decided to cook him lamb. And having seen a bottle of Jack Daniels in his office, the brothers bought a bottle of Jack to serve him as well. "We were brownnosing a little," Nariman laughed, "opening the door for his wife and whatnot. When the dinner was over, Bill said, 'Boys, that was the best steak I've ever had.' Then his wife laughed and told him it was lamb. He didn't like lamb. So he said, 'If you can make lamb taste that good, we are in business.'"

The business did well and eventually the banker gave the brothers the loan. Their second location in Abilene was opened in 2007 when partner Aaron Perez joined Nariman with the restaurant. They have been widely recognized in numerous publications for their chicken fried steak.

"My background was in French cuisine," Nariman shared. "In those first days when we were cleaning up the restaurant in Albany, a little old lady named Edith

Gwen came in. She said that she used to make chocolate and coconut pies for the café before it closed and asked if she could bring us some pies the next day for consideration. We said we weren't dessert eaters, so it was perfect for her to do her pies.

"The next day, she came back with her pies. I asked her about what chicken fried steak was, and she said, 'Oh you're in for a schoolin'! Y'all come to my house and I'll show you how to make it.' And she did. She showed us the way grandma makes it, the old-fashioned way. And that's the way we serve it."

If you've been to the Beehive, it's notably decorated with dollar bills that have names on them. Nariman said that, at the original restaurant, a hunter came in from New York City. He had a bar where the World War II soldiers would gather. They put their name on a dollar and put it on the wall before they went to war. "If you came back from the war, you could keep your dollar," Nariman shared. So that gentleman was the first one to put a dollar up and start the tradition. "Then, when we opened in Abilene," says Nariman," a guy came in and said it's not the Beehive unless there's a dollar on the wall. So he put the first dollar up and others followed."

photo by Tiffany Harelik

Turkey, Dressing, and Gravy

Ellen Webb via Carol Dromgoole, Albany/Abilene

"This is a combination of recipes from my mom and well-known Albany cook Josephine Williams," said Ellen. "I don't want anyone's dressing but Mom's," said Carol. This recipe is reprinted with permission from *You'll Be Going Back for Seconds* by Ellen Webb.

20–22 pound turkey
1 onion, sliced
2–3 ribs celery
7–10 chicken bouillon cubes
salt, to taste
pepper, to taste
butter

Dressing:

3–4 packages corn bread mix
10–12 slices bread
2 cups chopped onion
2 cups chopped celery
3–4 eggs, beaten
2 sticks margarine
salt and pepper to taste
sage to taste

Thaw and wash turkey thoroughly; slice onion and place inside turkey cavity with celery ribs. Put butter, salt, and pepper generously inside and out. Tie wings to turkey breast. Place in roaster. Place piece of cheesecloth over breast to keep breast moist. Add small amount of water to bottom of roaster and add 4 to 6 bouillon cubes. Cover and bake at 325° for 3½ to 4 hours or until tender. Baste occasionally. Remove on rack and place on cookie sheet to cool. Cover with foil to prevent drying.

Bake corn bread according to directions. Toast bread slices, both sides, until dry. Sauté onions and celery in butter until tender. Cook livers, gizzards, heart, and neck in enough water to cover. Add onion slices, celery ribs, 3 to 4 bouillon cubes, margarine, salt, and pepper and cook until tender. Set aside to cool. Crumble corn bread and toast. Add sautéed celery and onions, with sage to taste. Use hot stock from turkey and giblets to moisten to desired consistency and let cool. Add the 3 to 4 beaten eggs to dressing and bake immediately or refrigerate until next day. Bake at 350° for 45 to 60 minutes or until set and brown.

Slice turkey and place on serving platter or on a foil-lined cookie sheet. Put a little broth over and cover. Reheat when ready to serve.

To make giblet gravy, finely chop livers and gizzards and add to broth with finely chopped boiled egg. Thicken to desired consistency. Add 1 to 2 teaspoons browning sauce for color.

Venison Bourguignon

Rebecca Conley via Brennan Vineyards, Comanche

photo by Rebecca Conley

Thanks to our friends from Brennan's for this amazing recipe utilizing Texas wine.

1 pound venison (backstrap or steak)
1 cup frozen pearl onions
¼ teaspoon pink salt
¼ teaspoon fresh ground black pepper
½ teaspoon brown sugar
6 tablespoons butter, divided
4 slices Pederson's natural farms bacon, sliced into several squares
1 package button mushrooms, sliced
3 garlic cloves, minced
fresh thyme, chopped
1 tablespoon tomato paste (no added salt)
½ cup dry red Texas wine
1 cup low sodium beef broth
2 tablespoons water
1 tablespoon all-purpose flour

Set out pearl onions and allow them to thaw. Cut venison into one-inch cubes. Pat meat dry with a paper towel. Sprinkle with salt and pepper.

Heat a Dutch oven or deep cast iron skillet over medium heat. Melt 4 tablespoons of butter in the pan. Add seasoned, cubed, venison meat to pan and brown evenly on each side. Remove venison from pan.

Add the sliced bacon squares to the pan and sauté for 2 minutes. Add mushrooms to the pan and sauté until brown, stirring occasionally so that mushrooms do not stick to pan. Add garlic, thyme, and brown sugar to pan and stir constantly for 1 minute.

Add tomato paste. Cook for 1 minute. Pour in 1 cup of dry red Texas wine, and bring to a boil. You will need to scrape the pan occasionally to loosen up the fond (browned bits). Cook until liquid has reduced by half. Add thawed onions and beef broth; bring to a boil. Cook for 2 minutes.

Combine flour and water in small bowl or cup. Whisk with a fork until smooth. Add the flour-water mixture to the pan and cook until the sauce has thickened slightly. Return browned venison to pan. Turn heat off and simmer, stirring occasionally, for 10 minutes. Serve over a bed of mashed potatoes, rice, or egg noodles.

Rebecca Conley

Rebecca Conley started her career in the fashion industry, working on contracts in Southeast Asia, primarily Hong Kong. "After a few years, my pursuits took me to New York City where I stayed until 2008," she said. "I came back to Texas and lived in Houston where I found my passion for wine, and then moved to Lubbock and completed a degree in Viticulture and Enology."

Now Rebecca is the director of marketing and sales at Brennan Vineyards in Comanche, Texas. "I handle all of our creative departments, from web design to labeling, and I am very involved in our product development," she said. "All things that feed into sales."

"My grandmother was a fabulous cook with a fearless outlook in the kitchen. While she was certainly someone who followed and shared recipes, she also famously experimented and created her own. I have a lot of her personality in the kitchen.

"I loved grilled and smoked meats," she shared about food from her childhood. "I grew up in a household that always had the pit fired up on the weekends. That greatly influenced my favorite meals. Smoked turkey from Greenburg is always a favorite in our house, as well as Tom Perini's recipe for beef tenderloin. Those are our two holiday staples."

photo by Tiffany Harelik

Venison over Noodles

Connie Kirkham, Cross Plains

This is a great way to cook venison for the whole family.

1 package egg noodles, cooked until tender
1 small venison roast, cut in bite-sized pieces
1–2 tablespoons olive oil
½ cup onion, chopped
½ cup green bell pepper, chopped
½ cup celery, chopped
2 cloves garlic, minced
oil, for roux
flour, for roux
½ cup beef broth

Sauté venison in olive oil and add onion, green bell pepper, celery, and garlic. Continue to cook on low until onions are clear.

In a separate pan, make a roux with a little oil and flour. Cook on low heat until light brown. Gradually stir in ½ cup beef broth slowly. Add venison and veggies. If roux thickens too much, add a little hot water or broth to thin it back down. Serve over noodles.

Venison Piccata

Erin Maloney Schroeder, Abilene

"You can omit the step with the milk if you are not worried about the gamey taste. This makes 3 to 4 servings." —Erin Maloney Schroeder

1¼ pounds tenderized venison (can use tenderloin/blackstrap; just slice against the grain in thin slices, ¼ inch or less thick)

2 cups milk, divided

½ cup flour

½ teaspoon salt

½ teaspoon pepper

¼ cup butter

¾ cup dry white wine

2 to 3 tablespoons lemon juice

¼ cup snipped fresh parsley

1–2 tablespoons capers, drained

In a shallow dish, combine meat and 1 cup milk. Cover dish with plastic wrap and refrigerate for 1 to 3 hours. Drain and discard milk. Add remaining 1 cup milk and let stand at room temperature for 1 hour. Drain. Pat dry with paper towels. (This is the step I don't do.)

Mix flour, salt, and pepper. Coat meat in flour mixture. In a large skillet, melt butter over medium-high heat. Brown meat on both sides. Add wine. Cook about 2 minutes. Put meat on heated platter. Add lemon juice, parsley, and capers to skillet. Reduce heat to medium. Cook, stirring constantly, about 2 minutes, scraping bottom and sides of skillet. Serve sauce over meat.

Wagyu Chicken Fried Steak

Jean McWilliams, Cross Plains

"The UF ranch has produced beef for the public for 139 years and is in the process of making it a better product over the years. We began with Hereford cattle for many years, incorporated the black cattle (Angus) for more tenderness and taste, and are currently adding full-blooded, registered Wagyu. We suggest using very little seasoning on the meat so you can enjoy the flavor and taste of the meat itself and not the spices." —Jean McWilliams

Take a tenderized round steak and remove the fat and membrane. Cut a medium piece of meat and soak in sweet milk. In an iron skillet, melt shortening to a high heat for frying (about 350°).

Mix several cups of flour in a pan and add salt and pepper. Fill a separate bowl with sweet milk. Dredge the steak in the flour, then in the milk, then back in the flour. Drop in the hot grease and listen for it to sizzle. Leave until lots of blood comes to the top of the steak and most of the flour is moist. Slide a spatula under the steak and turn it to the other side to brown evenly on both sides. It should be a light brown.

White cream gravy (a must):

    4 tablespoons grease
    4 tablespoons flour
    2 cups milk
    salt
    pepper

Use grease from frying the steak. Be sure and leave some of the crust and brown pieces in the pan, and cook the grease with the flour until you have a tan-colored paste. Whisk in 2 cups of milk and cook on high heat for 3 to 6 minutes until the gravy thickens. Cook it longer if needed to get it thicker, keeping in mind it will get thicker as it cools.

DESSERTS

Hundred-Dollar Cake
The Texas Cowboys' Christmas Ball, Anson

AA's One-Egg Cake
Jean McWilliams, Cross Plains

Apricot Pie
Hailie Harelik Hubbard,
Comanche/Brownwood

Apple Pie
Hailie Harelik Hubbard,
Comanche/Brownwood

Best Peanut Butter Bars
or Balls
Jessica Melson, Abilene

Blueberry Mold
Doris Jackson via Gavin Jackson, Abilene

Bread Pudding
with Whiskey Sauce
Dr. Jimmy Harelik, Comanche/Cross Plains

Buttermilk Pie
Margaret Sherrod via Emily Gilmore, Abilene

Chessa's Cheesecake
Ellen Webb via Carol Dromgoole,
Albany/Abilene

Cherry Crumble Pie
Patricia Pickens, Abilene

Doris's Quick Chocolate
Pound Cake
Jessica Melson, Abilene

Everybody's Favorite
Pecan Pie
Dalya Hight, Aspermont/Old Glory

Foster's Chocolate Cake
Paulette Foster, Cross Plains

Foster's Pie
Paulette Foster, Cross Plains

French Coconut Pie
Roxie Thomas, Cross Plains

Gigi's Sour Cream
Pound Cake
Whitney Kirkham Henderson, Cross Plains

Grown-Up Milk and Cookies
Brennan Vineyards, Comanche

Linda's Fresh Carrot Cake
Linda Caldwell, Coleman

Oatmeal Caramelitas
Julia Porter Bramblett, Abilene

Paulette's Cookies
Paulette Foster, Cross Plains

Pumpkin Chiffon Pie with
Gingersnap Crust
Elmo Joy Wilson Ferguson, Hamlin,
via Martha Minter Ferguson

Red Velvet Cake
Angie Wiley, Abilene

Ruth Bonner's Fresh
Coconut Cake
Jean McWilliams, Cross Plains

Strawberry Shortcake
Perini Ranch Steakhouse, Buffalo Gap

Sugar Cookies with Icing
Tiffany Prier Lamb, Abilene

Tea Cakes
Maggie Meers, Hamby

Tommy's Spotted Pup
(Rice and Raisin Pudding)
The Texas Cowboys' Christmas Ball, Anson

Texas Gold
Whitney Kirkham Henderson, Cross Plains

Hundred-Dollar Cake

The Texas Cowboys' Christmas Ball, Anson

This recipe by Rhonda Weaver was printed with permission from the TCCB Association members from the *Texas Cowboys' Christmas Ball Ranch Supper Cookbook*.

1 cup sugar

2 cups flour

4 tablespoons cocoa

1½ teaspoons baking soda

1½ teaspoons baking powder

1 cup cold water

1 cup Miracle Whip

2 teaspoons vanilla

Icing:

1 cup sugar

¼ cup cocoa

¼ cup milk

¼ cup butter

Mix together sugar, flour, cocoa, baking powder, and baking soda. Add the rest of the ingredients and mix well. Bake in two 9-inch round cake pans or one 9x13 sheet pan. Cook at 350° for 25 to 30 minutes or until center springs back when pressed. Cool before icing.

To make the icing, bring all ingredients to a boil in a pot on the stove. Set aside to cool. Stir while cooling until it reaches a spreadable consistency.

AA's One-Egg Cake

Jean McWilliams, Cross Plains

When Jean shared this recipe with me, she said she didn't know why AA called it a one-egg cake, because the recipe calls for two eggs. "AA always had this cake for the buyers that came to the ranch on 'delivery day.' Buyers would come to the ranch to look and go through your steers to take the best ones to go to the feedlots, as well as young age heifers for replacement heifers for cows. This was a big day with buyers, hoping they buy all the cattle for a once-a-year paycheck (and usually turned very few down)."

1½ cups sugar
½ cup Crisco
2 eggs, separated
2¼ cups cake flour
1 cup milk
3 teaspoons baking powder
1 teaspoon salt
1½ teaspoons vanilla

Beat sugar and Crisco together. Add egg yolks, one at a time. Add flour and milk (a little of each, alternating as you are mixing them in). Beat egg whites and fold into the cake batter along with remaining ingredients.

Caramel icing:

½ pint cream
2 cups sugar
⅔ cup brown sugar
6 tablespoons butter
1 tablespoon vanilla
1 cup pecans

Heat sugar, and as it turns brown, pour in cream slowly and stir continually. Pour back in pan or cool until you have a soft ball (don't overcook). Remove and add butter, vanilla, and pecans. Beat and spread on cake. The icing should be creamy and soft, not sugary. For birthday cake, AA would add a pineapple filling instead of the caramel icing.

Pineapple filling:

2 tablespoons butter
2 tablespoons flour
½ cup sugar
1 egg
1 cup pineapple juice

Melt butter and add remaining ingredients until thick. Start with the flour, sugar, and egg, then add the juice.

This can be used for the filling in between the cakes and a seven-minute icing can be used to ice the built cake on the outside.

Apricot Pie

Hailie Harelik Hubbard, Comanche/Brownwood

Cook's note: For the pie crust, I prefer to roll my dough out between two sheets of wax paper.

Pie crust (makes 2):

- 2½ cups flour
- 1 tablespoon sugar
- 1 tablespoon salt
- 1 cup vegetable shortening
- 6–8 tablespoons ice water (I usually use 8+ depending on what it takes to get it just moist enough)

Combine all dry ingredients; add shortening in small chunks and cut in with a knife or pastry dough cutter until pieces are pea-sized. Add water a few tablespoons at a time until it all begins to stick together without overly crumbling. Don't overmix and don't add too much water. Separate into two balls, wrap in plastic wrap, and refrigerate a minimum of one hour and up to two days.

Apricot filling:

- 1½ pounds of dried apricots
- 4 cups water
- ⅓ cup sugar
- ½ teaspoon cinnamon
- ¼ teaspoon ground cloves
- dash of nutmeg
- 2 tablespoons butter

Set pie dough out to soften. Preheat oven to 425°. Add dried apricots and water to saucepan, and simmer for about an hour until apricots are soft and have absorbed most of the water. Mash apricots to desired consistency. Add sugar and spices; mix using a wooden spoon. Set aside to cool.

Line pie plate with rolled-out dough. Carefully pour in apricot mixture. Dab evenly with butter. Roll out second pie crust, center over apricots, seal edges, and crimp. Cut slits in the top crust. Place pie plate in a shallow pan in case some juices seep over. Bake 45 minutes or until pie is golden brown, including the bottom pastry. If the top browns too quickly, add a sheet of foil to the top.

Apple Pie

Hailie Harelik Hubbard, Comanche/Brownwood

photo by Ariane and Jaqueline Peveto

"You can fine-tune and adjust as you wish. I've never written it out, so it may be a bit scattered."

Cook's note: For the pie crust, I prefer to roll my dough out between two sheets of wax paper.

Pie crust (makes 2):

2½ cups flour
1 tablespoon sugar
1 tablespoon salt
1 cup vegetable shortening
6–8 tablespoons ice water (I usually use 8+ depending on what it takes to get it just moist enough)

Combine all dry ingredients, add shortening in small chunks, and cut in with a knife or pastry dough cutter until pieces are pea-sized. Add water a few tablespoons at a time until it all begins to stick together without overly crumbling. Don't overmix and don't add too much water. Separate into two balls, wrap in plastic wrap, and refrigerate a minimum of one hour and up to two days.

Filling:

    1 cup sugar
    4 heaping tablespoons flour
    pinch salt
    ⅛ teaspoon ground cloves
    ¼ teaspoon pumpkin pie spice
    1 teaspoon cinnamon
    pinch ground ginger
    2 pounds apples (I prefer to mix half Fuji or Gala with half Granny Smith)
    1 tablespoon lemon juice
    2–3 tablespoons butter

Preheat oven to 425°. Set out cold pie dough to soften. Roll out one pie crust to line the bottom of pie plate; set aside. Core, slice, and peel apples. I prefer to cut my slices into chunks as well. Add lemon juice and toss in a large bowl. In another bowl, combine all dry ingredients using a whisk. Pour over apple bits and toss. Let sit and marinate for a few minutes to allow juices to mix.

Transfer apple mixture to prepared pie plate. Apples should be heaping in a mound (it will bake down). Add small dabs of butter evenly all over apples. Roll out second pastry dough, place evenly over apples, seal edges, and crimp. Cut slits in the top crust. Place pie plate in a shallow pan in case some juices seep out. Sprinkle the top of the pie with cinnamon and sugar if desired. Bake 45 minutes until apples are tender and juices are boiling.

photo by Ariane and Jaqueline Peveto

Best Peanut Butter Bars or Balls

Jessica Melson, Abilene

This is a traditional holiday recipe for my family. We make them into balls dipped in chocolate at the holidays, and the kids and carpools are always super excited when we do bars topped with chocolate for an after-school snack.

- 2 cups peanut butter
- 1 cup brown sugar
- 2 sticks of butter or margarine
- 1 teaspoon vanilla extract
- 1 box of powdered sugar (about 3 and ¾ cups)
- 1 bag chocolate chips

Melt over low heat peanut butter, butter, and brown sugar. Stir in vanilla extract when the mixture is melted and combined. Slowly stir in powdered sugar until combined. Remove from heat.

Pour into 9x13 pan and smooth or roll into balls. If you're leaving them in the pan, sprinkle chocolate chips over the top and melt under broiler just until soft and melted. Remove and smooth with spatula. Flash freeze or place in the refrigerator to set. If you're rolling them into balls, melt chocolate chips in the microwave and dip each ball, and then flash freeze or refrigerate to set.

Jessica Melson

"I'm an RN but currently a personal driver for my three children," shared Jessica. She has moved eight times to different states and never moved back to a particular state, but she has called the Big Country her home for the last twelve and a half years.

She considers asking Jesus into her heart at age twelve, playing college basketball, marrying Joe Melson, having her first child three months early, and moving to Abilene as some of her greatest moments.

"Poppy seed chicken when I came home from college" was one of her favorite family meals "and peanut butter balls at Christmas."

Jessica said that Perini Ranch Steakhouse is always a special place for her family to celebrate. "Our youngest even at seven would choose Perini's over pizza places for his birthday meal. Catfish and ribs!

"Abilene is overall a caring, philanthropic community like none other. Always giving and supporting those in our city."

Blueberry Mold

Doris Jackson via Gavin Jackson, Abilene

Doris suggests using this as a spread on raisin bread—toasted or plain. This recipe yields about ten servings. You may wish to reserve a few fresh blueberries as an optional garnish.

Combine and stir until dissolved:

> 1 large package blueberry gelatin
> 1 cup boiling water

Add:

> 1 can Musselman's blueberry pie filling
> 1 can crushed pineapple, drained
> ½ cup chopped pecans

Pour into a 5-cup mold and chill until firm. For an optional topping, combine and blend:

> 1 8-ounce package cream cheese
> 1 cup sour cream
> ½ cup sugar
> 1 teaspoon vanilla
> dash salt

Bread Pudding with Whiskey Sauce

Dr. Jimmy Harelik, Comanche/Cross Plains

You can replace the French bread with day old bread if you have leftover bread from yesterday's dinner.

    1 loaf French bread
    1 quart milk
    2 eggs
    2 cups sugar
    2 tablespoons vanilla
    3 tablespoons margarine, melted
    1 cup raisins (I use currants)

Soak bread in milk. Crush mixture with hands until well mixed. Add eggs, sugar, vanilla, and raisins; stir well. Pour margarine in bottom of thick pan and cover with the bread mixture. Bake until firm in a 350° oven, approximately 45 minutes. Let cool. Cube pudding and put in individual dessert dishes. When ready to serve, add sauce and heat under broiler.

Whiskey sauce:

    1 stick butter or margarine
    1 cup sugar
    1 egg
    whiskey to taste

Cook sugar and butter in double boiler until very hot and well-dissolved. Add well-beaten egg and cook very fast so egg doesn't curdle. Let cool and add whiskey to taste.

Buttermilk Pie

Margaret Sherrod via Emily Gilmore, Abilene

"Both my husband Trey's and my grandmothers make buttermilk pies. We love this version in our home." —Emily Gilmore

    1 9-inch unbaked pie shell
    ½ cup butter
    1½ cups sugar
    3 tablespoons flour
    3 eggs, beaten
    1 cup buttermilk
    1 teaspoon vanilla

Preheat oven to 350°. Melt butter and let cool. Add sugar and mix well. Add flour and eggs; beat well. Stir in buttermilk and vanilla. Pour into unbaked pie shell. Bake at 350° for 45 to 50 minutes. Cool on wire rack before serving.

photo by Emily Gilmore

Chessa's Cheesecake

Ellen Webb via Carol Dromgoole, Albany/Abilene

This cheesecake serves 10 to 12. This recipe is reprinted with permission from *You'll Be Going Back for Seconds* by Ellen Webb.

Blend:

> ¼ cup margarine or butter
> 1 package graham crackers, crushed

Line 9x13 buttered dish with crumbs. Save a few for the top. Chill a large mixer bowl and beaters.

> 1 large can and 1 small can evaporated milk—chill until almost frozen
> 1 8-ounce package cream cheese
> 1 cup sugar
> juice and zest of 1 lemon
> 1 package lemon Jell-O
> 1 cup hot water
> 1 teaspoon vanilla

Mix Jell-O and water and cool, but do not let congeal. Cream together and chill cream cheese and sugar. Set aside.

Pour milk into cold mixing bowl. Start beating on high and when milk starts to fluff, add lemon juice. Continue beating until bowl is almost full. Add cream cheese mixture by thirds, then add cool Jell-O gradually. Add vanilla as you add Jell-O.

Pour immediately into chilled dish. Sprinkle remaining crumbs on top. Cover with plastic wrap sprayed with nonstick spray to prevent sticking and refrigerate immediately. Serve with whipped cream.

Ellen Webb

"My dad, Sam Webb, was a longtime insurance agent in Albany. His family was one of the founding families in the town. Webb Park (the city park) is named for the family. My dad, now deceased, was a first cousin to John Matthews, of the Matthews/Lambshead ranching families.

"My mother turned ninety-five in July 2016. She was honored the previous fall as the oldest Marine in Abilene. She joined the Marines during World War II and served as a stenographer and secretary in Quantico, Virginia, at the War College (I think).

"Mom grew up on a farm in Mexia, Texas. That's where she learned to cook. Her dad would be working the farm. During the Depression, her mom took a job in town, so mom learned to cook for everyone at an early age." —Carol Dromgoole (Ellen's daughter)

Ellen recommends Perini Ranch Steakhouse and Fort Griffin General Merchandise (the Beehive) in Albany for great local restaurants. She said she always loved cooking. "I always helped prepare meals for special events at Matthews Memorial Presbyterian Church in Albany," said Ellen.

Cherry Crumble Pie

Patricia Pickens, Abilene

photo by Crystal Johnson

"This is my son Clinton's favorite." —Patricia Pickens

Graham cracker crust:

1¼ cups graham cracker crumbs (put graham crackers in ziplock bag and smash); these are better than bought crumbs

¼ cup of sugar

¼ cup melted butter (or more as needed to get the crumble to come together, up to ½ cup)

Mix crumbs and sugar together; stir in melted butter. Place mixture in glass pie dish. Using the back of a spoon, press into the bottom of the pan and up the sides. If the pie dish is large or sides are high, you may need to double the mixture. I usually do because I like a thick crust. Bake for 10 minutes at 350° just to get the crust set.

Cherry pie:

21 ounces of cherry pie filling

1 tablespoon cornstarch

1 tablespoon water

Crumble mixture:

¼ cup sugar
¼ cup light brown sugar, packed
⅔ cup flour
⅔ cup quick-cooking oats
6 tablespoons melted butter

Preheat oven to 375°. Mix water and cornstarch in small bowl to make a paste. Put cherry pie filling in another larger bowl; add the paste and gently mix paste into pie filling. Pour this filling mixture into pie shell. If you use a larger pie dish, you may want to double the pie mixture in order to make a nice full pie.

Mix ingredients for the crumble. (I always double this: what I don't use on the pie, my family eats. It is their favorite part.) This mixture will be moist and clumpy. I drop little clumps all over the cherry pie. The pie should be completely covered, with no red showing through.

Bake at 375° for 35 minutes. If you have extra crumble mixture, bake on a cookie sheet, stirring often. This extra will not take as long to cook as the pie. Cool at least 4 hours. Serve at room temperature.

Patricia Pickens

Patricia Pickens shared an explanation of where the Big Country is located: "Look at a map of Texas. Put one index finger on El Paso, now put the other on the northeastern corner of the Panhandle. Slowly drag those fingers toward the center of the state. Where they meet in the middle: that is Taylor County. It's not technically called Central Texas, but it seems the most central to me."

Patricia's parents were from the area surrounding Abilene. "My grandfather was a chemistry professor at Hardin-Simmons University, and my father was a doctor in Abilene for many years," she said. She considers her children two of her greatest accomplishments: "Amy, my oldest. Also, Clinton, who is so very talented and charismatic."

"My mom encouraged my sisters and me to cook," she said, "and it seemed easy because you just had to follow directions. That is what I have always liked about cooking: there are instructions. You do one thing, then you do another, and if you do it right, you get what you're after . . . then over time you get to play around with it and experiment to come up with your own dishes.

"The recipe I submitted is a family favorite. I try to bake it whenever both kids are in town. The house is full when we are all together, because there is a son-in-law now, and grandbabies, cousins, nieces, nephews, girlfriends, and of course grandparents and even great-grandparents running around. It is literally and figuratively full. It's the figurative that I love. When my house is full with family my heart is full. One of my favorite things is to see my kids standing over my pie, picking apart the crust (which they joke is like a drug) and laughing and talking and sharing stories. It doesn't even bother me that they destroy the crust; besides, I normally make two pies and hide one till dinnertime.

"The Big Country is a great place. There are genuine people here," shared Patricia. "It's a close-knit community full of good people. One aspect of the community that is very important to me is how the people here have been a part of my faith. There are a lot of jokes about how there is a church on every corner in Taylor County, but the truth is (for me) that this part of the world has been a place to plug into a community of believers through my church. It's a freedom that I have here and I don't take it for granted."

"The Big Country has always been home. I've raised my children here and seen friends and families come and go. Food is a big part of the culture, but you need both. When I look back at the moments that make me happiest, they're both there. The people and the food. People make food, but company makes food taste better. The excitement of getting dressed up and driving out to Buffalo Gap for a steak. Picking our son up at the airport and letting him choose his favorite Abilene spot to have dinner. The sound of my grandkids playing outside on a hot summer day; laughing and yelling all while the droning motor of the homemade ice cream tumbler is providing the background music and anticipation of what's to come. That makes me smile."

Doris's Quick Chocolate Pound Cake

Jessica Melson, Abilene

photo by Tiffany Harelik

"This is my mother-in-law's chocolate pound cake that we just cannot get enough of. New neighbors get this treat delivered warm when we go to meet them." —Jessica Melson

1 yellow cake mix
2 small chocolate instant pudding mixes (3.9 ounces each)
4 eggs
½ cup oil
1¼ cup water
1 bag chocolate chips (we use semisweet, but Doris likes milk chocolate)

Preheat oven to 350°. Combine eggs, oil, and water until thoroughly mixed. Add to the cake mix and blend with mixer until well combined. Stir in chocolate chips. Pour into an oiled and floured Bundt pan. We use two 6-cup Bundt pans so that a neighbor gets one and we get one. Bake at 350° for 1 hour if using one Bundt pan or 35 minutes with two smaller pans.

Everybody's Favorite Pecan Pie

Dalya Hight, Aspermont/Old Glory

Dalya's pecan pie is a must-have at any Big Country Thanksgiving table.

    4 eggs
    ⅔ cup sugar
    ⅔ cup light Karo syrup
    1 teaspoon vanilla
    a dash salt
    1–2 tablespoons melted butter
    ½ teaspoon caramel flavor
    1½ cups pecans
    1 unbaked Pillsbury rolled piecrust

Preheat oven to 350°. Beat eggs. Stir in other ingredients one at a time. Pour ingredients into the unbaked pie shell.

Bake at 350° for 45 to 50 minutes until crust is golden brown and pecan mixture is set.

Dalya Hight

Dalya Hight was born at home, seven miles north of Old Glory. "A doctor from Rule made house calls and was there to deliver me. You couldn't tell my name from what he wrote on the paper, so my parents had to change it at the courthouse," shared Dalya. Her grandfather, Solon Johnson, and his eventual father-in-law, Reese Fuston, were among the first to homestead Old Glory in the 1880s.

"I started school in Old Glory, but I went to Aspermont High School my junior and senior years after lots of invitations from the superintendent. I don't know why I did that because I was always so bashful. I graduated in 1951 with a graduating class of around twenty-five people."

Dalya played basketball in high school. She remembers: "They made us play baseball in PE and I didn't like to—my aversion became even stronger when one of my fingers was broken by a stray baseball." Her senior trip to Mexico was a fond memory from high school.

"I married in '53, had three kids, became a Christian in 2006—that took a long time," Dalya shared. In addition to being a mother of three, she was a hardworking housewife and worked in the Farm Bureau Office.

"In 1957, my husband was working on an oil rig in Post, Texas. They would stop in at a local café there. He kept talking about the pecan pie and how great it was, so I decided to go taste it and see what all the fuss was about. After having a piece, I guessed that they were using more eggs in their recipe, so from that day forward, I began putting four eggs instead of three in my pecan pie. It makes it a little less sweet and syrupy."

About the Big Country, Dalya said, "Everyone is friendly in these small towns—they're willing to help each other in any way they can."

Foster's Chocolate Cake

Paulette Foster, Cross Plains

This is a tried and true Foster family recipe from Callahan County.

Wet ingredients:

1 cup water
2 sticks margarine
½ cup buttermilk
2 eggs, beaten
1 teaspoon vanilla

Dry ingredients:

2 cups flour
2 cups sugar
4 tablespoons cocoa
1 teaspoon baking soda

Preheat the oven to 425°. Melt the margarine with the water over low heat to combine. Pour the remaining wet ingredients in the pot with the margarine and water to combine thoroughly.

Mix the dry ingredients together thoroughly. Combine the wet and dry ingredients and pour in a cake pan. Bake for 20 minutes on 425°.

Icing:

4 tablespoons cocoa
1 teaspoon vanilla
1 stick margarine, melted
1 pound powdered sugar
¼ cup milk

Mix all ingredients together. Spread fresh icing onto the cake while the cake is still warm.

Foster's Pie

Paulette Foster, Cross Plains

This family recipe has simple ingredients that you likely have on hand, making it easy to make on short notice.

1 cup pecans, broken
1 cup light Karo syrup
1 cup sugar
3 eggs
½ teaspoon flour
1 unbaked pie shell

Mix all ingredients and pour into a pie shell. Bake at 450° for 30 minutes or until pie browns. Once it has started to brown, turn the heat down to 200° and bake another 20 minutes.

French Coconut Pie

Roxie Thomas, Cross Plains

photo by Richard Fonvielle

"This pie is my go-to recipe for church potlucks and family lunches. It's quick to assemble and always a hit. A shallow 9-inch pie pan works best." —Roxie Thomas.

1 stick butter, melted
1½ cups sugar
3 eggs, beaten well
1 tablespoon vinegar
1 teaspoon vanilla
1 cup shredded coconut
1 unbaked pie shell

Preheat oven to 350°. Mix all ingredients well, making sure sugar is thoroughly incorporated. Pour into pie shell and bake for one hour. Allow to cool and set before serving.

Roxie Thomas

Roxie Thomas graduated from Cross Plains High School in 1978 in a graduating class of forty-eight. She played volleyball and basketball and was involved with the student council.

"I retired from banking three years ago (in 2013) after thirty-three years of service. I'm currently being caregiver for my grandson in Dallas," she said.

When I asked Roxie what were some of the major events in her life, she said, "Marrying a terrific man, raising our children in a small town. Although we raised our kids in a small community, we encouraged them to venture out and explore large cities where they could obtain a higher education.

"We have been blessed to live in a community where lifelong friends live. We have attended grade school through high school with these people and raised our children together. We now celebrate our grandkids.

"My family comes from the Glen Rose and Granbury area. My paternal grand-father was a rancher and owned the acreage used to build the Comanche Peak Nuclear Power Plant. My maternal grandfather was a rancher and dozer operator. He was instrumental in digging Lake Granbury. My dad's coaching career and farming and ranching brought us to this area. We moved to the community of Nimrod (outside of Cisco) when I was nine. My dad and his cousin farmed peanuts together. My sister, brother, and I knew what it was to move irrigation pipe, clear stumps to create farmland, hoe peanuts, and sew sacks of peanuts in the field. We worked but also had time for fun. We had a variety of pets from our country living, including a fox and an owl.

"Both my grandmothers were excellent cooks. I always enjoyed cooking and trying new recipes because of them. Thanksgiving and Christmas found us at my grandmother Mamaw's table. She cooked so many things that there were two large rooms to venture into to fill your plate. Desserts were always abundant and exceptional. Chicken and dressing was always made on any holiday."

About her community, Roxie says, "Cross Plains is a loving, caring community. When a need arises, whether it be monetary or time, the people respond."

Gigi's Sour Cream Pound Cake

Whitney Kirkham Henderson, Cross Plains

"Gigi was my grandmother Alice Santleben Roby. This recipe was handed down to Gigi from her mother Opal Santleben." —Whitney Kirkham Henderson

- 2 sticks butter
- 3 cups sugar
- 6 eggs, separated
- ¼ teaspoon baking soda
- 1 cup sour cream
- 3 cups flour
- 1 teaspoon vanilla extract
- 1 teaspoon almond extract

Cream together butter, sugar, and egg yolks. Beat until creamy. Separately, stir baking soda into the sour cream. Add flour and sour cream alternately into creamed mixture. Add flavorings.

Beat egg whites until stiff peaks form and fold into batter. Put in greased and floured tube pan. Bake at 300° about 1 hour and 20 minutes.

Whitney Kirkham Henderson

"I live in Coleman County. I moved twelve miles away from my home place," said Whitney Henderson. "I have lived in the Big Country basically my whole life. I did live near Austin when my oldest son was born, but I decided that I wanted to raise my children in the same small town that I grew up."

She lives on her husband's grandfather's home place. "It is known around Coleman and surrounding areas as the 'Henderson Place,'" said Whitney.

Whitney graduated from Cross Plains High School where she participated in basketball, track, and cheerleading. "There were thirty-six kids in my graduating class, and it was a big class for Cross Plains!" said Whitney. "I have so many great memories growing up—so many people around Cross Plains that made me who I am today. I still see and get to hug several of my grade school teachers; they know my children and they tell them the best stories."

I asked Whitney what is something she wanted people to know about her community. She said, "I truly believe that if more people were like those in Cross Plains—what a different world we would live in. Our community as a whole knows what it is to take care of our own. If something needs to be done, we do not wait for someone to come and do it for us. We join together and get the job done. People in our town remember what pride is like for your country, and they live accordingly. I was raised and continue to raise my children with the old saying of God and country.

"My mother (Connie) was raised on ranches her whole life, and my grandmother instilled that style of country cooking in her. My mom always cooked. On rare occasions, my dad would fix us scrambled egg sandwiches.

"My grandmother became foreman of the Weldon Edwards Ranch after my grandfather died. She was filmed on television in the '80s, and the anchorwoman asked her if she ever had trouble finding good help. She answered, 'No, because I am a good cook.' Needless to say, she passed on her cooking skills to my mother, and I was lucky enough to learn from them both. So, my husband never has trouble finding help when needed!"

Whitney also started a program for children in Cross Plains. "Jeremiah 29 is a nonprofit program that feeds low income children during the summer months to ensure they receive a warm meal every day. We feed approximately twenty-five to thirty kids a day during the summer months. This program receives all of its funding from individuals in or connected to Cross Plains. No big government grants, just people wanting to make a difference in a kid's life," which she says is another reason why Cross Plains is so special.

Grown-Up Milk and Cookies

Sheila Wells of Brennan Vineyards, Comanche

photo by Rebecca Conley

"Got leftover Tempranillo? Cabernet? Super Nero? Don't throw it out! Make cookies—you won't be disappointed. Serve with a glass of Brennan's award-winning Lily Reserve." —Sheila Wells

    3 cups all-purpose flour
    1 teaspoon baking powder
    ½ cup chopped almonds (or pistachios—whatever you have)
    5 tablespoons granulated sugar
    1 cup dry red wine
    ½ cup canola oil
    extra sugar for rolling dough into "sticks"

Preheat oven to 350°. In a large bowl, combine the flour, baking powder, and sugar. Add the wine and oil. Mix with a dough hook attachment or just get your hands in there and get to work! Take out your frustrations!

Form into sticks about 4 inches long and ½ inch in diameter (think "breadstick"). Roll in extra sugar. Place on ungreased cookie sheet. Bake for approximately 20 minutes. Cookies should be hard and crisp.

Linda's Fresh Carrot Cake

Linda Caldwell, Coleman

Farm-fresh carrots make this cake even more special.

2 cups sugar
4 eggs
1½ cups vegetable oil
3 teaspoons cinnamon
2 teaspoons baking soda
1 teaspoon salt
2 cups flour
2 tablespoons vanilla
3 cups carrots, grated

Preheat oven to 325°. Mix and blend sugar, eggs, and oil. Mix cinnamon, soda, salt, and flour, then blend in with batter. Mix in vanilla and carrots.

Grease and flour three round cake pans. Bake at 325° for 30 minutes. Let the cake set before removing from pan. Use the frosting to ice the layers between the cakes and the top layer.

Frosting:

1 stick butter
1 8-ounce package cream cheese
1 cup pecans
1 box powdered sugar

Combine all ingredients and mix thoroughly until blended.

photo by Cathy Allen

Catherine Caldwell Allen (Cathy)

"I have lived in Coleman County (better known as God's Country) all my life, with the exception of the time I spent in Lubbock after high school. I graduated from Texas Tech and moved back home, and that's when I really became involved with our family business—Owl Drug."

Cathy graduated from Coleman High School and participated in track, basketball, and the drill team. There were sixty-five kids in her graduating class. "The kids we grew up with and went to school with were like brothers and sisters to me," shared Cathy. "We knew everyone's name and graduated with many of the kids we started kindergarten with."

When I asked Cathy what she would like for people to know about her community, she said: "We have one of the best small-town public libraries you'll ever see, a great rodeo in June, and a Christmas parade. We are friendly, rural, casual, laid-back, western, and traditional, and we have a hunter's and fisherman's paradise, and we are surrounded by beef lovers!

"My husband's side of the family has been in this area for six generations in the land and cattle ranching industries. The recipe for the Rafter 3 Beans is an old family recipe that originated on the ranch and is a family favorite. It was used by the wagon cooks when the cowboys were out on the ranch.

"My mother's side of the family has been in this area for four generations, mostly in the pharmacy business. Both of my mother's parents were pharmacists and had a pharmacy in Santa Anna, Texas. Mom's brother and only sibling is also a pharmacist. My father's family was also in the pharmacy business. Dad's only brother is a pharmacist, his father was a pharmacist, and his mother manages the store (Owl Drug in Coleman, Texas)," shared Cathy.

"All the women in my family love to cook and they are fantastic chefs! My grandmother Opal Riley, one of the first female pharmacists in Texas, and I had so many wonderful times in the kitchen together when I was a child . . . she was an amazing cook! She was retired, and my brothers and I spent lots of time with her while we were growing up! I can still taste her iron skillet fried chicken with homemade mashed potatoes and gravy. She made everything taste so good! I learned the love of cooking from 'Meemaw.'

"My mother Linda is also a pharmacist, and as such, she is a wonderful, health-conscious cook and has always prepared the most delicious and fresh, healthy meals. Mom is organized and focused in the kitchen and has always had a palate for adventure! I learned the pleasure of diversity from all kinds of foods and spices in Mom's kitchen! Both of these women inspire me with their passion in the kitchen and especially the fact that they would cook three meals a day almost every day, to make sure our bodies were properly nourished."

Her mom's nachos were one of her favorite meals: "Mom would make these perfect nachos—each chip was meticulously its own piece of art!"

Oatmeal Caramelitas

Julia Porter Bramblett, Abilene

Julia was born in Dallas and grew up in Abilene. She says she loved making this recipe with her mom, and now all her kiddos love making it with her.

Crust:

2 cups flour

2 cups oats

1½ cups firmly packed brown sugar

1 teaspoon baking soda

½ teaspoon salt

1¼ cups butter, softened

photo by Cassie Knapp-Abeln

Filling:

8 ounces chocolate chips

8 ounces peanut butter chips

½ cup chopped pecans

12-ounce jar of caramel ice cream topping

1 tablespoon flour

Preheat oven to 350°. Grease a 13x9 pan. In a large bowl, combine all crust ingredients with a hand mixer at a low speed, until crumbly. Press half of the crumb mixture (about 3 cups) into the bottom of the greased pan. Save the remaining crumb mixture for the topping. Bake for 10 minutes.

Sprinkle the chocolate and peanut butter chips and pecans over the warm crust. Combine the caramel topping with the flour and drizzle evenly over the chips and pecans. Sprinkle the remaining crumbs from the crust mixture on top. Bake an additional 18 to 22 minutes or until golden brown. Cool completely for 1 to 2 hours. Cut into bars and serve.

Paulette's Cookies

Paulette Foster, Cross Plains

photo by Crystal Johnson

Easy to make, you will love having these cookies fresh out of the oven. This recipe yields 2½ dozen cookies.

    1 cup butter, room temperature
    ⅔ cup brown sugar
    1 egg
    2 cups flour
    1 teaspoon vanilla
    1 teaspoon cinnamon, optional

Preheat oven to 350°. Mix all ingredients, and make into very small balls. Place on a greased cookie sheet. Press down with a fork. Bake at 350° or up to 400° on some ovens for 10 minutes.

Pumpkin Chiffon Pie with Gingersnap Crust

Elmo Joy Wilson Ferguson, Hamlin, via Martha Minter Ferguson

"Truly a delicious alternative to the ordinary pumpkin pie . . . made by the best cook in all of Jones County!" —Martha Minter Ferguson

Blend 1 tablespoon unflavored gelatin and ¼ cup water; set aside. Mix together in saucepan:

> ¾ cup brown sugar
> ½ teaspoon salt
> 2 teaspoons cinnamon
> ½ teaspoon ginger
> ½ teaspoon allspice
> 1⅓ cups canned pumpkin
> 3 large egg yolks
> ½ cup whole milk

Cook over low heat until boiling; boil one minute. Stir in softened gelatin. Let cool. When partially set, beat until smooth. Carefully fold in meringue:

Meringue:

> 3 egg whites
> ¼ teaspoon cream of tartar
> ½ teaspoon vanilla
> 6 tablespoons sugar

Let the egg whites stand at room temperature for half an hour before working with them to add volume to the meringue. Beat egg white, cream of tartar, and vanilla until the mixture forms soft peaks. You can do this by hand or with an electric mixer on medium speed. Add the sugar one tablespoon at a time. If you add the sugar too quickly, it will take away the fluff from the egg whites and ruin the meringue. Continue to beat until you have glossy peaks.

Gingersnap crust:

> ¼ cup butter, melted
> ½ cup gingersnap crumbs (about 18 gingersnaps)

Mix crust ingredients; press into 9" pie pan. Bake 10 minutes at 325°. When cool, fill with pie mixture. Chill overnight; garnish each piece with whipped cream.

Red Velvet Cake

Angie Wiley, Abilene

photo by Tiffany Harelik

Although red velvet cake is considered a Southern tradition by many, the recipe actually has its roots in New York City, with the Waldorf-Astoria claiming stakes to the original recipe. There are many variations to this cake. The reaction of the vinegar and buttermilk combination pulls a red color out of the cocoa, and some cooks even use a beet mixture to help with the red color. But during the Depression, Adams Extract (based in Texas) was the first to sell red food coloring, which assisted cooks in achieving an even deeper red. The coloring lends its name to red velvet, but it is also called devil's food. The traditional icing is a French-style butter roux, although cream cheese and buttercream frostings are also used.

"This is the real deal. My grandmother made this for my birthday every year. It is a real benefit to have an automatic stand mixer." —Angie Wiley

Cake:

1 cup shortening
1½ cups sugar
½ cup sour cream
3 eggs
1 teaspoon vanilla
1 teaspoon butter flavoring
3 tablespoons cocoa
1½ ounces red food color

photo by Tiffany Harelik

2½ cups sifted flour

1 teaspoon salt

1 cup buttermilk (whole, not low-fat, is best but not critical)

1 tablespoon vinegar

1 teaspoon baking soda

Get the frosting started, so the ingredients cooked in the first step have time to cool.

Then cream shortening, sugar, sour cream, eggs, vanilla, and butter flavor. Make a paste of cocoa and red color and blend in to the creamed mixture. Combine salt with sifted flour, then add flour/salt combination and buttermilk alternately to the batter. Mix baking soda and vinegar in a small bowl and blend into the batter.

Spray three 9 or 10 inch round pans, then flour. Bake cakes in the round pans for 20 minutes at 350°, checking at 15 to be sure they do not cook too long, making the cake dry. Let cool completely, remove from pans, and layer with frosting between each layer.

Frosting:

2 cups milk (whole milk is best, but not critical)

6 tablespoons flour

1 teaspoon salt

2 cups shortening

2 cups sugar

4 tablespoons vanilla

½ teaspoon butter flavor

coconut flakes needed to cover iced cake

Cook milk, flour, and salt in a saucepan, stirring constantly until thick. Let cool.

Cream shortening and sugar very well. Blend in vanilla and butter flavor. Combine with the first mixture and beat well until fluffy and smooth. Layer cakes with icing in between, then cover the stacked layers with remaining icing. If desired, cover whole cake with coconut.

Ruth Bonner's Fresh Coconut Cake

Jean McWilliams, Cross Plains

"Ruth was our father's mother, and she always made this on Christmas and Easter."
—Jean McWilliams.

  1 cup Crisco
  2 cups sugar
  ½ cup milk
  ½ cup coconut juice
  3 cups cake flour, divided
  2 teaspoons baking powderpinch salt
  8 egg whites

Cream Crisco and sugar. Add ½ cup of flour and milk. Add coconut juice and rest of flour that is sifted with baking powder and salt. Last, fold in egg whites that have been beaten to peaks. Bake in three layers at 350° for approximately 15 minutes. Do not overcook.

Filling:

  3 cups sugar
  1 cup water
  ½ cup coconut juice
  3 egg whites, beaten
  1 14-ounce package grated coconut
  1 cup whipping cream

Boil sugar, water, and coconut juice until it spins a thread. Pour over egg whites that have been beaten to stiff peaks and beat well. When partly cool, add grated coconut. Refrigerate; whip cream to peaks and when frosting is cold, fold in.

Put icing in between cake layers and on outside layer of cake before serving.

Strawberry Shortcake

Perini Ranch Steakhouse, Buffalo Gap

photo by Tiffany Harelik

Reprinted from *Texas Cowboy Cooking* from Tom Perini with permission from Tom and Lisa Perini (pages 179 and 141).

"This is another recipe from my great-grandmother, Mrs. Becky Blake from Abilene. With the Texas biscuits and the warm strawberries, it's just to die for." —Tom Perini

2 pounds fresh ripe strawberries
½ cup sugar
8 buttermilk biscuits, sweetened to taste
1 cup heavy cream

Remove the tops from the strawberries and cut in half. Sprinkle with the sugar and let sit at room temperature until they begin to juice. Put the strawberries and juice in a saucepan and over very low heat, warm thoroughly until the juice begins to thicken. Split the biscuits and scoop strawberries onto biscuit bottoms. Replace top and cover with another spoonful of strawberries. Top with heavy cream. Serves 8.

Buttermilk Biscuits

These were definitely a staple in the early ranch and chuck-wagon days, but we still eat them all the time. In fact, we serve them every Sunday with the Judge's Fried Chicken. The sourdough biscuits were more common on the wagons. Later, when buttermilk was accessible at the cookshack, with some form of refrigeration and milking cows nearby, buttermilk biscuits were used. There are, of course, other kinds of biscuits like the hardtack, which is a flat, hard, unleavened biscuit. These are both pretty simple to make and are delicious with everything from cream gravy to butter to fresh peach preserves.

2 cups flour
2 teaspoons baking powder
½ teaspoon baking soda
¾ teaspoon salt
3 tablespoons vegetable shortening
1 cup buttermilk

Combine the dry ingredients. Add the shortening and mix well with the back of a mixing spoon. Add the buttermilk and mix thoroughly. Roll out dough on a floured board to a ½-inch thickness. Cut into rounds and place on an ungreased baking sheet. Bake at 450° for about 10 minutes, or until browned. Makes 24 biscuits.

Sugar Cookies with Icing

Tiffany Prier Lamb, Abilene

photo by Tiffany Harelik

This is Mrs. Judy Voelter's recipe—my mom's—and it makes 5 to 6 dozen.

1 cup Crisco

2 cups sugar

2 eggs

⅔ cup milk

2 teaspoons vanilla

½ teaspoon salt

1 teaspoon cream of tartar

1 teaspoon baking soda

5 cups all-purpose flour

Mix all ingredients together in order—mixing after each cup of flour. After mixed well, roll out on counter and cut out into desired shapes. Bake for 6 minutes at 350°.

Icing:

1 cup Crisco

1 pound powdered sugar

1 teaspoon vanilla

1 teaspoon almond extract

pinch salt

4 tablespoons water

Mix well and add food coloring as desired.

Tea Cakes

Maggie Meers, Hamby

photo by Catherine Thomas

"This is my great-grandmother's recipe (Dorothy Bennett of Lueders, Texas). They are perfect for Christmas cookies! We have used this recipe for years." —Maggie Meers

    1 cup sugar
    ½ cup shortening
    2 eggs
    ½ teaspoon grated lemon peel
    1 teaspoon vanilla
    2 teaspoons baking powder
    2 cups sifted flour
    ½ teaspoon salt

Preheat oven to 350°. Cream sugar and shortening well. Add eggs and flavorings (lemon peel and vanilla). Sift dry ingredients (baking powder, flour, salt) and fold in mixture.

Bake at 350° on greased cookie sheet for 5–10 minutes right before they turn golden brown.

Tommy's Spotted Pup
(Rice and Raisin Pudding)

The Texas Cowboys' Christmas Ball, Anson

This recipe by Tommy Spraberry was printed with permission from the TCCB Association members from the *Texas Cowboys' Christmas Ball Ranch Supper Cookbook*.

2 cups cooked rice

1½ cups sugar

½ teaspoon salt

½ teaspoon cinnamon

½ teaspoon nutmeg or allspice

⅓ cup raisins

4 eggs

2 cups milk

⅓ teaspoon cocoa (optional)

Mix dry ingredients and add eggs and milk. Cook at 350° for 45 minutes or until firm.

Whiskey sauce:

½ cup whiskey

½ teaspoon vanilla

powdered sugar to thicken

Mix and heat ingredients together over medium heat, stirring frequently for 1–2 minutes until the sugar is dissolved.

Texas Gold

Whitney Kirkham Henderson, Cross Plains

photo by Sassafras Company

"This is a Henderson family favorite." —Whitney Henderson

    1 box yellow cake mix
    1 stick butter, melted
    3 eggs, divided
    4 cups powdered sugar
    8 ounces cream cheese, softened

Preheat oven to 300° and spray a 9x13 dish with cooking spray. In a large bowl, mix cake mix, melted butter, and one egg into soft dough. Press into bottom of the pan. With a hand mixer, combine powdered sugar, softened cream cheese, and remaining two eggs until smooth, about 1 to 2 minutes. Pour on top of dough, and smooth. Bake at 300° for 40 to 50 minutes until top is golden brown.

photo by Sassafras Company

photo by Tiffany Harelik

Author: Tiffany Harelik

Born in Austin, raised in Buffalo Gap, Tiffany Harelik is Texas to the bone. The former Sweetwater Rattlesnake Round-Up Queen has explored the world over, capturing backstories from the backcountry and recipes from the range in efforts to preserve recipes and culinary cultures. From her first project, *The Trailer Food Diaries Cookbook Series*, to her more recent titles including *The Big Bend Cookbook* and *The Terlingua Chili Cookbook*, Tiffany is on the cookbook road trip of a lifetime. Her books combine a quirky cast of characters with heirloom recipes in her trademark anecdotal style. Look for exciting new up and coming titles at www.tiffanyharelik.com.